Australian BUSH PUBS

XXXX
TELSTRA PREPAID
I
PUB

Australian
BUSH PUBS

A CELEBRATION OF OUTBACK AUSTRALIA'S ICONIC WATERING HOLES

CRAIG LEWIS & CATHY SAVAGE

www.boilingbilly.com.au

www.woodslane.com.au

THE FAMILY HOTEL
VICTORIA BITTER
STAR BAR

WEST END
FAMILY HOTEL
COMING SOON
GEORGIE AT THE FAMILY
SINGING AND KARAOKE
SAT 6TH SEPT
FROM 6PM
PUBSTAY

SHOP
Careys corner
PLEASE BE PATIENT
WHAT HAPPEN'S NEXT
MELBOURNE BITTER
Campervan Motorhome Club
JIM BEAM
BLOW JOB
A DRINKING PROBLEM
BE REASONABLE DO IT MY WAY
JACK LIVES HERE
HIGHEST
Ford
Peace Love Happiness

This book is for all, both past and present, who have stood at the bar of one of Australia's greatest outback institutions — the bush pub.

Contents

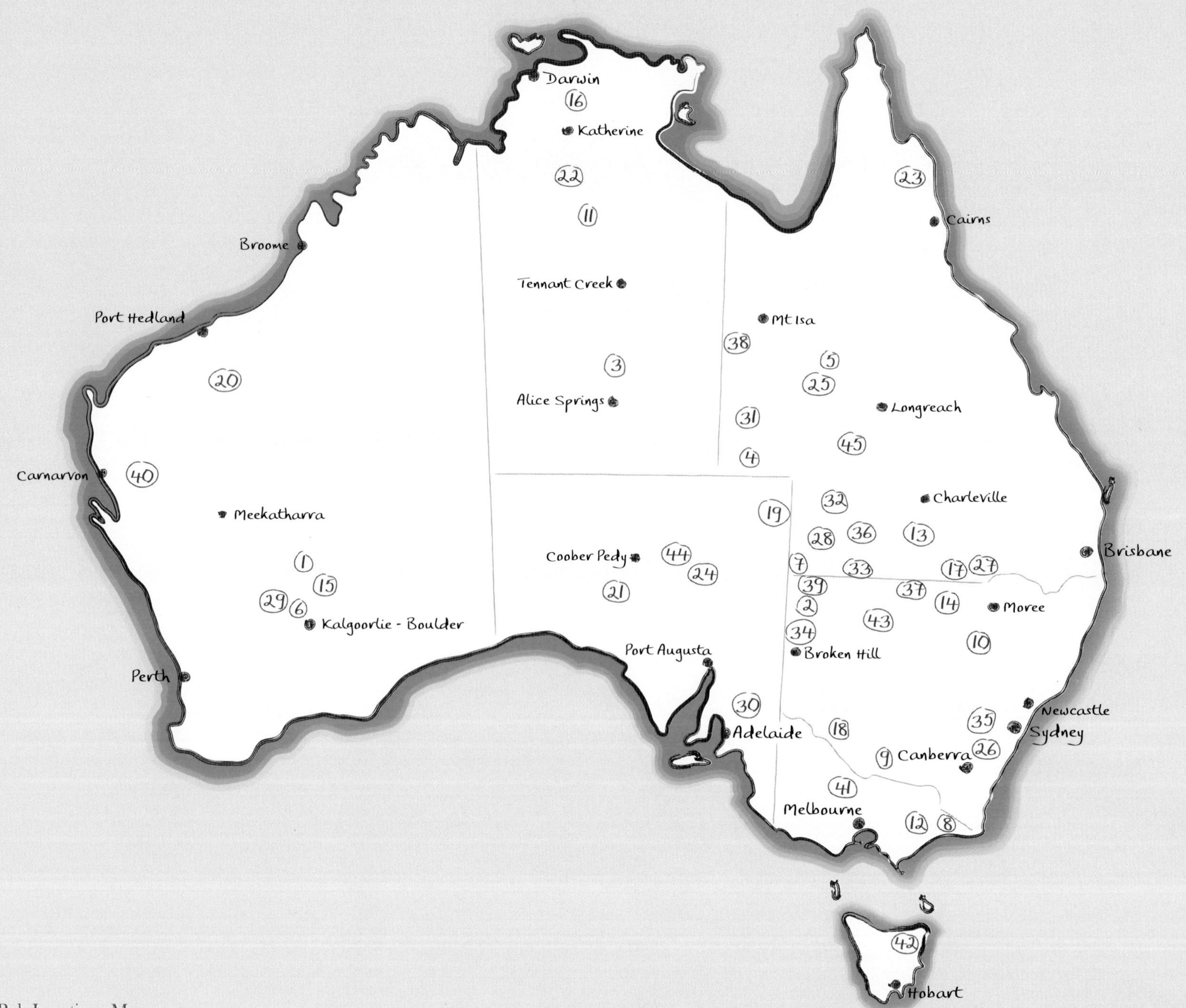
Darwin
16
Katherine
22
11
23
Cairns
Broome
Tennant Creek
Port Hedland
Mt Isa
38
5
25
20
3
Alice Springs
Longreach
31
45
4
Carnarvon
40
Meekatharra
19
32
Charleville
28
36
13
Coober Pedy
44
24
Brisbane
1
7
33
17
27
15
39
37
14
Moree
29
6
21
2
Kalgoorlie - Boulder
43
34
10
Port Augusta
Broken Hill
Perth
30
Newcastle
35
Adelaide
18
Sydney
26
9
Canberra
41
Melbourne
12
8
42
Hobart

Pub Locations

1 Agnew Hotel - WA
2 Albert Hotel - NSW
3 Barrow Creek Hotel - NT
4 Birdsville Hotel - QLD
5 Blue Heeler Hotel - QLD
6 Broad Arrow Tavern - WA
7 Cameron Corner Store - QLD
8 Commercial Hotel - VIC
9 Conargo Hotel - NSW
10 Cuttabri Wine Shanty - NSW
11 Daly Waters Pub - NT
12 Dargo Hotel - VIC
13 Gladstone Hotel - QLD
14 Glengarry Hilton - NSW
15 Grand Hotel - WA
16 Grove Hill Hotel - NT
17 Hebel Hotel - QLD
18 Homebush Hotel - NSW
19 Innamincka Hotel - SA
20 Ironclad Hotel - WA
21 Kingoonya Pub - SA
22 Larrimah Hotel - NT
23 Lions Den Hotel - QLD
24 Marree Hotel - SA
25 Middleton Hotel - QLD
26 Nerriga Hotel - NSW
27 Nindigully Pub - QLD
28 Noccundra Hotel - QLD
29 Ora Banda Inn - WA
30 Overland Corner Hotel - SA
31 Royal Hotel - Bedourie QLD
32 Royal Hotel - Eromanga QLD
33 Royal Mail Hotel - QLD
34 Silverton Hotel - NSW
35 Sofala Royal Hotel - NSW
36 South Western Hotel - QLD
37 Tattersalls Hotel - NSW
38 The Dangi Pub - QLD
39 The Family Hotel - NSW
40 The Junction Hotel - WA
41 The Logan Pub - VIC
42 The Pub in the Paddock - TAS
43 Tilpa Hotel - NSW
44 William Creek Hotel - SA
45 Yaraka Hotel - QLD

Introduction

Australia's bush pubs are an integral part of our social fabric; woven with colourful characters that helped shape our vast and remote areas, well away from the hustle and bustle of the cities. Like many of our well known landmarks, these humble establishments too are icons, many having stood the test of time when they once served almost frenetic metropolises that are today little more than ghost towns. In the enduring outback spirit, many of these cornerstones of the bush are still dispensing their own unique brand of hospitality.

The pubs within these pages are a selection of both iconic outback drinking spots, many of which have played a role in our folklore heritage, along with a scattering of classic, although lesser known bush hotels. We need to stress here that this is by no means a complete rundown of every bush pub to be found throughout Australia. That would be a monumental task in itself, and one which would severely punish our livers (which, by the way, copped a hard enough time as it was with this lot).

When we set out to write and photograph this book our aim was to document bush pubs as they are today, though many have survived for well over a century. Over the last 15 or so years that we've been travelling through the backblocks we've seen a steady decline in the number of bush pubs; many having shut their doors for one reason or another. So we reckoned that a record of one of our great outback institutions was needed. It's partly a history book, partly travel guide and partly photographic journey to some of our best loved bush watering holes. You may agree or disagree with some of our choices, or even reckon we've missed out on a great bush pub. If this is the case please drop us a note (you'll find the address towards the back of the book) and we may well look at these in another edition.

Many of our featured pubs stem from the goldrush days when towns sprung into existence literally overnight. Some towns boasted almost an obscene number of pubs and illegal grog shanties relative to their populations, but more often than not these were short lived and only the hardy survived. Kookynie's Grand Hotel and Milparinka's Albert Hotel are good examples. Other hotels were once part of the web-like stage coach network which criss-crossed much of eastern Australia. The best known of these firms was Cobb & Co who used these establishments to stable fresh horses and provide meals and accommodation for their travel weary passengers. Middleton Hotel and Hungerford's Royal Mail Hotel are relatively authentic reminders of these glory days of coach travel.

Some bush pubs are rather elaborate affairs, considering their locations. Take the impressive Marree Hotel, a handsome two storey sandstone structure which once served the bustling railway town on the edge of the desert. These days things are much quieter in Marree, and the hotel looks almost out of place, standing sentinel against a vast desert backdrop. One the other hand, Grove Hill and Larrimah hotels are simple buildings constructed of recycled material like steel pipe and corrugated iron, which reflects their locations as much as their purpose. However, all of the bush pubs featured have one thing in common: character.

The unsung heroes of bush pubs are the publicans who keep the tradition of bush hospitality alive and well. The Tattersalls Hotel's Mary Crawley (now well into her 80s) has been serving behind the bar of her hotel for over 30 years, while the Commercial Hotel's Graham Beever has been keeping the drinks coming for more than 20 years in his Victorian pub.

From us, thank you to all the publicans whose pubs are featured in this book, you welcomed us and without hesitation let us wander around collecting information and taking photographs.

Cheers,

Rocky Hall, New South Wales

CARLTON
DRAUGHT
BREWERY FRESH
HOTEL & MEALS

A

Agnew Hotel

Albert Hotel

Agnew Hotel

Situated in Western Australia's 'dry and desolate' northern goldfields, the Agnew Hotel has been quenching the thirsts of the region's parched gold miners since the 1950s.

Agnew Hotel
Campbell Street, Agnew
Western Australia
(08) 9037 5929

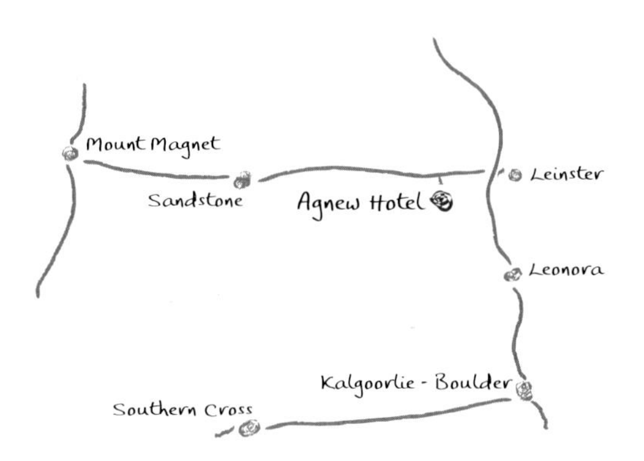

The Angew Hotel was one-time utilised as a haberdashery store, a post office and garage in the nearby town of Lawlers.

Relocated to the new mining settlement of Agnew sometime in the 1930s, the timber and corrugated iron buildings then served as a butcher shop and tea rooms in this bustling shanty town.

Agnew, much like Lawlers, was plagued by mining accidents and declining gold yields. By 1948, just twelve years after being gazetted as a town, the school closed as the town's population continued to dwindle.

In 1954 a local man by the name of Bill Cock purchased a row of four shop fronts in the town and then went about refurbishing the dilapidated buildings, with their American 'wild west' styled store fronts, into the hotel. There's still one of the old butcher fridges being used beneath the hotel's front bar.

Agnew had thrived during most of its life with illegal gambling and sly grogging keeping the miners entertained. Legend has it that the Agnew Hotel wasn't actually licenced until 1975!

Mining resumed in Agnew in the 1980s, and during the intervening years it was only the hotel which saved Agnew from becoming extinct.

Today, apart from the hotel, little of old Agnew remains. The mine's work force now lives in nearby Leinster or they fly-in fly-out, however the Agnew Hotel is still well patronised by the local miners, but it's not so much the rough and tumble of the mining days of old.

AGNEW
HOTEL

Albert Hotel

A gold rush to far western New South Wales in the late 1870s saw Milparinka proclaimed a town in 1880. The Albert Hotel is the last remaining hotel of four that once thrived in this outback post.

Albert Hotel
Main Street, Milparinka
New South Wales
(08) 8091 3863

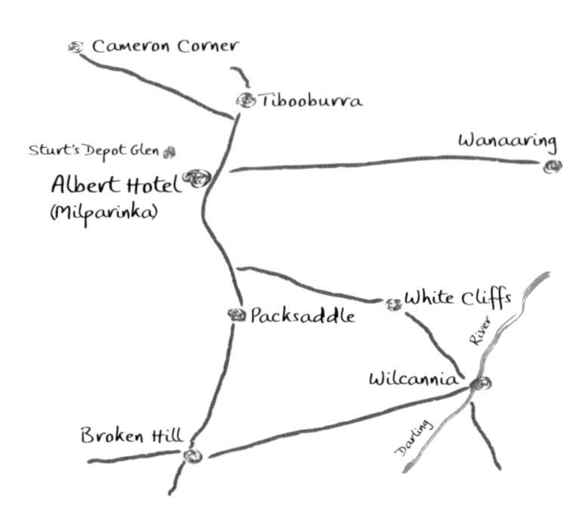

In March 1882 a publican's licence was granted to a Mr Patrick Kenny for a public house to serve the burgeoning goldfields of the state's far north-west. To be called 'The Albert', this, like many of the town's more substantial buildings, was constructed of local sandstone.

In 1890 the then owner of The Albert, Mr George Blore, built an additional stone building at the rear of the hotel to house race horses for the upcoming Christmas meet. Other publicans of note include Mr William Baker, who in June 1893 was charged for retailing from a licenced premises – he had sold a bag of sugar.

In 1897 Mr Thomas Hill became publican. It was during his time that the hotel came to the attention of local police. The Albert was marred by fighting, stealing and illegal selling of liquor.

Today, the front section of the Albert Hotel is what remains of the original structure, albeit in a renovated form. A walk through the front bar takes visitors into an internal courtyard with a fish pond – this area being surprisingly cool even during the warmer months. Located off this courtyard are a number of original guestrooms, with room six apparently haunted by the ghost of a young lady.

Regularly frequented by shearers, prospectors and travellers, there's certainly some interesting yarns to be had in the pub's front bar.

OPEN

Sydney Electricity

Milparinka Gold

When Milparinka was first proclaimed a town, there were also three other towns in the vicinity; Mt Browne, Albert and The Granites. Aside from Milparinka, only The Granites, later changing to its Aboriginal name of Tibooburra, remains.

Miners came to the region on foot, walking over 300 kilometres to the fields with pick, shovel and miner's right in hand. The lack of water was a major issue for miners, although mining continued in the area until the early 1920s. At this time public buildings such as the post office, school and courthouse closed – this was the beginning of the end of the town of Milparinka.

Captain Sturt's Expedition

Some 35 years prior to the proclamation of Milparinka the area was visited by veteran explorer Charles Sturt on his expedition to find the fabled inland sea.

Located to the north-west of the Albert Hotel, Depot Glen is a permanent waterhole where Sturt and his team were forced to camp for six months whilst waiting for rain to allow their retreat south to settled areas.

Sturt had his men build a rock cairn on the nearby hill, which he named after his second in command James Poole, who died during the expedition's enforced stay. He is buried to the east of Depot Glen.

A tent township numbering almost 500 men grew beside a waterhole on Evelyn Creek as gold fever gripped the region.

The four saddest words
that were ever
composed,
THE BAR IS CLOSED
XXXX The Classic Aussie beer
You are in SHEEP COUNTRY
Eat Mutton You Bastards
A Million Bloody Dingoes Can't Be Wrong !!
EULO QUEEN HOTEL - EULO
Far South Western Queensland
Lake Macquarie
NOBBYS
CARLTON & UNITED BREWERIES
303
Icegold
375mL
FOXTRAP
COOLADDI S.W.QLD.
"I'll Meet You There"
hard earned thirst
BEER!
HELPING UGLY PEOPLE
HAVE SEX SINCE 1862
XXXX
LIGHT BITTER
Chill ou
For a hard earned thirst.
VICTORIA

XXXX
The Classic
Aussie beer

XXXX
LIGHT BITTER

POWER'S
NATURALLY BREWED
BITTER
345ml

PRIORITY
COUNTRY AREA
PROGRAM

Fast-forwarding

CARLTON
MID
DOUBLE
HOPPED
BITTER BEER

BEER!
MAKES YOU SEE DOUBLE
MAKES YOU FEEL SINGLE

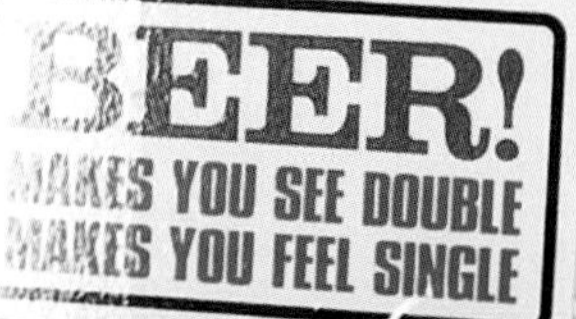

XXXX
LIGHT BITTER

B

Barrow Creek Hotel

Established in 1932, this unique bush pub stands beside the Stuart Highway, offering refreshments to the hordes of travellers who ply the road between Alice Springs and Tennant Creek.

Barrow Creek Hotel
Stuart Hwy, Barrow Creek
Northern Territory
(08) 8956 9753

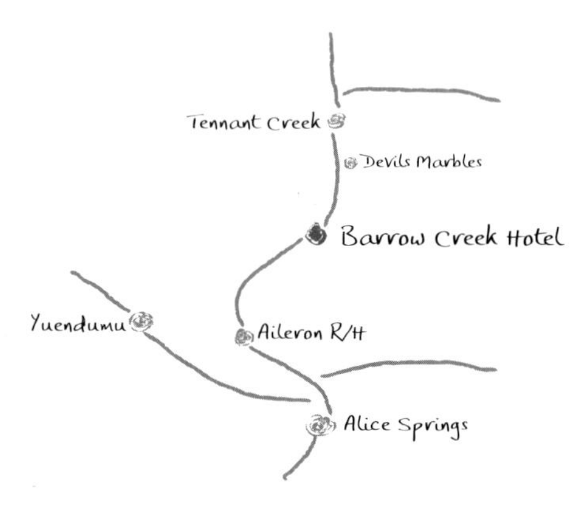

Walking into the front bar of the Barrow Creek Hotel is like stumbling upon an oasis in the desert, especially if you're thirsty. Just about every nook and cranny in this place is plastered with some form of memorabilia (or pubobilia). There are road signs, hats, pictures, money in numerous denominations along with thousands of signatures adorning all available space. You could spend hours reading comments scrawled by travellers who have passed this way.

Built by the enterprising Kilgariff brothers out of hand-made concrete blocks, the hotel served its first drink on November 4th 1932 and before long was catering to the increasing number of travellers undertaking the adventurous journey along the old unsealed Stuart Highway.

Tom Roberts, affectionately known as the 'Mayor of Barrow Creek' worked at the telegraph station next door to the pub for almost 40 years, and was one of the hotel's colourful characters.

Station hands and droving teams where also regular visitors to the Barrow Creek Hotel. It was the ringers from these teams that initiated the tradition of pinning their last note with their name on it to the roof and walls of the hotel. This ensured that they had enough money to buy a drink on their next visit – a tradition that has continued to the current day with notes from around the world pinned to the walls of the hotel. Although it doesn't look like many people take their money down – it stays pinned to the walls as testament to their visit to Barrow Creek.

EXIT
YARCK HOTEL
Wrangler
BACON & EGGS
CEREAL, TOAST & CUPPA
SAUSAGE, LAMB CHOP,
EGGS & GRAVY
STEAK, EGG & ONIONS
EGGS (POACHED OR SCRAMBLED)
SPAGHETTI OR BAKED
TOASTED S'WICHES FROM
HOT CHIPS
FISH & CHIPS
VEGIE BURGER
N/A
15.00
8.00
7.00
5.00
4.50
11.00
N/A
STEAK
CHEESE
BULLSHIT
TODAYS
PLEASE
I CAN ONLY PLEASE ONE PERSON PER DAY AND TODAY IS NOT YOUR
No Smoking
TAB

BARROW CREEK
EST. 1932
HOTEL
BARROW CREEK HOTEL
EST 4TH NOV. 1932
STAFF ONLY
XXXX
MRS MAC'S
FAMOUS BEEF PIES

Into The Night

Images of the Barrow Creek Hotel were beamed around the world when the sleepy wayside inn bolted to prominence on Sunday July 15, 2001 after a road train pulled up out the front of the hotel in the early hours of the morning, the driver waking publican Les Pilton. Sitting terrified in the truck's cab was young Joanne Lees.

Joanne Lees recountered her experience of being attacked, bound and gagged by a solitary man who had stopped her and her partner, Peter Falconio along the Stuart Highway further north. It wasn't until later that day that the story hit the news headlines that Peter Falconio was missing.

Lees explained how Falconio had gone to the back of their van and spoke to the man. She then heard a loud bang and was attacked. Neither she or anyone else have ever seen Falconio again.

After an extensive man-hunt lasting 13 months, which stretched across the country, police apprehended a suspect in August 2002.

On December 13, 2005 Bradley John Murdoch was found guilty of the murder of Peter Falconio and was sentenced to life imprisonment with a 28 year non-parole period. To date Peter Falconio's body has never been found.

The pub at Barrow Creek is of architectural heritage value as being the first hotel built along the Stuart Highway.

Birdsville Hotel

Lying at the northern end of the Birdsville Track, the Birdsville Hotel is without doubt Australia's most famous bush pub, and has become ingrained in outback folklore.

Birdsville Hotel
Adelaide Street, Birdsville
Queensland
(07) 4656 3244

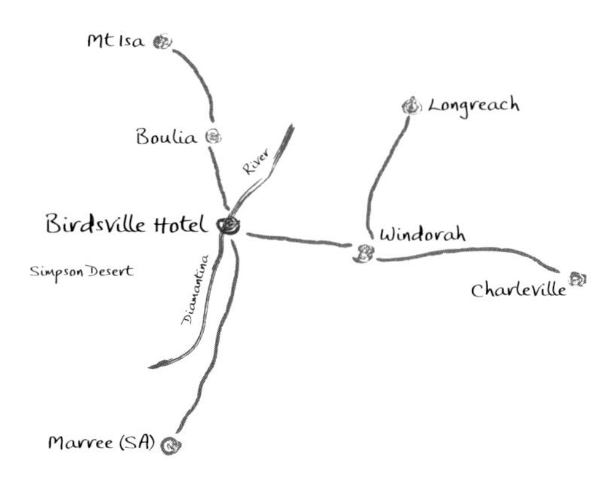

Birdsville is about as remote as a place gets, standing since 1884 on the edge of the vast Simpson Desert, Australia's last untamed frontier. The hotel is forged into Australian folklore and travellers now make their pilgrimage to one of Australia's treasured icons, just as drovers, ringers and outback wanders have done for over a century. As they say, you haven't had a beer in the outback until you've had a beer at the Birdsville Pub!

These days the pub is a mecca for travellers, many whom make the run up the once infamous Birdsville Track from Marree, about 500km to the south. Originally a stock route used by cattle drovers, the track is now a reasonably well-maintained road, but it still has the allure of the outback, as does this legendary pub.

Birdsville was first established as a stopover for drovers in the early 1880s. A customs post was erected soon after and before long the hotel came into existence. The original section of the hotel, which still stands, was built from whatever local rock could be found, including numerous small gibbers. These thick walls have some very uneven edges, but this just adds to the pub's appeal. The walls are whitewashed and often take on a gorgeous yellow glow as the late afternoon sun sinks into the Simpson Desert.

Inside, the pub is bursting with atmosphere. Dotted around the walls in the front bar are memorabilia and photographs, there's also the collection of hats above the bar.

XXXX
BIRDSVILLE CUP
XXXX
XXXX
XXXX
MOTEL
BOOKINGS HERE
STANDING
ANY TIME
ZONE
NO SMOKING
TAKEAWAY
ALCOHOL
MUST BE PURCHASED
BEFORE MIDNIGHT
& OFF THE PREMISES
BY 12.30 am
AKUBRA
HATS
$170
for sale in reception
PLEASE
RING BELL
XXXX GOLD

ESTABLISHED
1884
BIRDSVILLE HO
PUBLIC BAR

EL

MARK
THE
UTTER UTTER
BASTARD
DANIEL
POLGLASE
Bill
KNIGHT
JOHN
BRYSON
Shane
CUFFE
Raymond
NICHOLLS
PATTO
Norman
HARRIS
2377
DOUG
ENSOR
(mid 1999–2002)
Bob
GOAD
Charlie
KIWI
BRIAN
HANNA

Green Lizard Room

Although most people head straight for the front bar of the famous pub, the hotel also boasts another bar. This is the oddly named Green Lizard Room.

According to former publican Mick Studdart, the Green Lizard Room was christened in honour of a cocktail made from Creme de Menthe. Studdart once told me the yarn on my first visit to the pub. Apparently late season rains had swept down from the Gulf Country, catching most towns in the Channel Country by surprise. Generally these remote outposts receive ample warning of impending wet weather, but this time the news came too late and literally overnight Birdsville and the surrounding districts were deluged with rain. The beer truck was due into town the following day!

The town ended up being cut-off for nearly a month, with essential supplies being flown in by light plane, landing on a levelled sandhill.

Within a week the pub was out of beer, then wine and rum until the only drink left were a few bottles of Creme de Menthe.

In the first week of September over 5000 rowdy race goers converge on Birdsville for the annual Birdsville Cup!

Blue Heeler Hotel

Named after Queensland's favourite working dog, the Blue Heeler Hotel was once one of three hotels in Kynuna. This delightful pub has been a favourite stop for thirsty travellers since 1889.

Blue Heeler Hotel
Matilda Hwy, Kynuna
Queensland
(07) 4746 8650

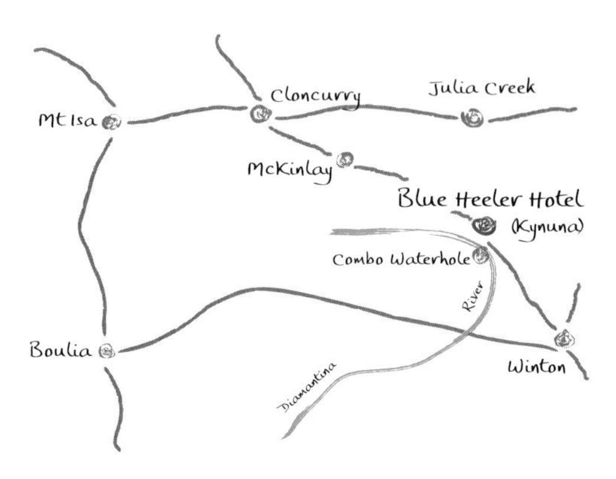

Originally known as Absolons Hotel, this timber weatherboard and corrugated iron hotel was built in 1889 and is still pretty much original. The large neon Blue Heeler on the roof was apparently a 99th birthday gift from the XXXX Brewery, and there's the large impressive fireplace that was built by the late RM Williams for the hotel's 100th birthday. Even with these newer additions the pub still retains much of its rustic charm.

This pub also played a role in one of Australia's best known songs. In 1894 Banjo Paterson visited the MacPherson family of nearby Dagworth Station. It was during a visit to the hotel that Robert MacPherson handed champagne through a pub window to the shearers outside. This gesture put to end the angry shearers strike of that year.

Paterson teamed this observation with the unrelated stories of the suicide of 'Frenchy' Hoffmeister and the drowning of another man in a billabong in the area.

Paterson then penned the words to a Scottish tune played on a zither by Miss MacPherson. The tune was 'Waltzing Matilda'. Paterson wrote of Waltzing Matilda shortly before his death; 'not a very great literary achievement, perhaps, but it has been sung in many parts of the world'.

The billabong in the song is believed to be the Combo Waterhole, which is located 20 kilometres east of The Blue Heeler Hotel.

Robert MacPherson abandoned Dagworth Station in 1930 due to drought and whilst at the then Absolons Hotel died from a heart attack.

BLUE HEELER
XXXX
POWER'S
NATURALLY BREWED
BITTER
"That's Better"

RUM
FIRE
1300 762 299
THE CREW
HEELER
MA SHADOW
LAUREN
2002
STEVO the DEVO
BIG DOG
DAN CAMERON
PLONKY & ANNETTE

Ph: 3855 1095
Mob: 0412 741 109
HEADS
TURNER
XXXX
XXXX
XXXX
XXXX
RoadKill
RoadKill
H.A.M.C
FAT MAN
Hells Angels
BRISBANE
PHIL
Matt Norrie 2/8/06
Dan "Sadsy" Sullivan
Tour 2006

VB
JOANNE DAWSON
SCOTTY HAKS & VAUGHN NEWMAN
HOPPER
KEEP ON
ALL SINGLE FEMALES
BE VERY WELCOME
BLACK STIX
WERE HERE
K.T.I
Boyz
waz
ere
on the
6.6.06
WE WAS ERE

WINTON SHIRE
McKINLAY SHIRE
COMBO WATERHOLE
2 MILES

BLUE HEELER
XXXX
BLUE HEELER
HOTEL
KYNUNA

Broad Arrow Tavern

The Broad Arrow Tavern is seen as something of a goldfield's icon. For over 100 years it has been providing beer, meals and a welcoming place for patrons to relax and unwind.

Broad Arrow Tavern
Railway Street, Broad Arrow
Western Australia
(08) 9024 2058

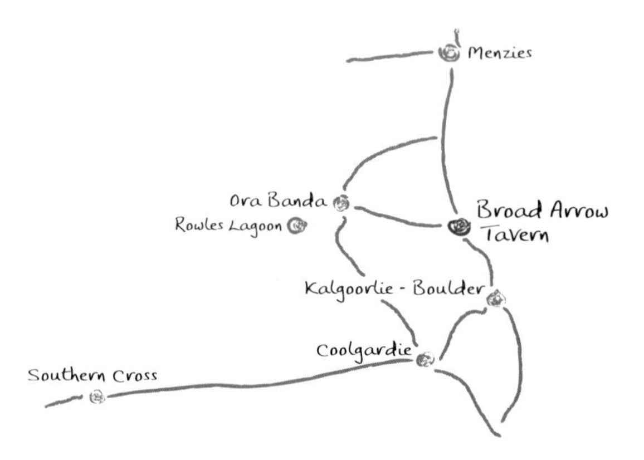

The corrugated iron clad Broad Arrow Tavern, or BAT as it is affectionately known, was established in 1896 and is the only surviving hotel, and indeed the only surviving business, from the town's heyday of 1900. Back then there were eight hotels, two breweries, two banks, a hospital, resident magistrate, stock exchange, and all the other associated businesses usually found in a town.

The town's two breweries, The Shamrock Brewery and the Broad Arrow Brewery were established in the late 1890s. Author Arthur Reid wrote in 1933 'that judging by the volume of beer brewed, Broad Arrow must have had the biggest beer drinking population in the world'.

Inside the BAT is a welcoming and very characterful front bar, a dining room off to the right and a pool room behind the bar. Every inch of the corrugated and weatherboard walls are signed by visitors, even the bar has signatures on its bright blue front. The dining room, however, has been saved from the permanent marker, its walls feature historic photos and articles of Broad Arrow and its surrounds.

In 1971 the hotel was featured in the movie, *The Nickel Queen*, the story of a female pub owner who stakes a mining claim on an area where nickel is found and who subsequently has an American company buy her out so she can live it up. The flick starred British actress Googie Withers and Australia's own 'Golden Tonsils' John Laws.

Nowadays Broad Arrow has a permanent population of six.

TAVERN
BROAD ARROW
TAVERN
EFTPOS

Whats in a name?

Apparently in 1893 a prospector by the name of O'Mara left Kalgoorlie telling his nephew he would leave a trail of broad arrows scratched on the ground, showing his direction of travel so that he could follow him later with a horse and cart.

Although Broad Arrow was the commonly used name, the town was first gazetted as Kurawah in 1896, and was officially changed to Broad Arrow in 1897.

With good gold finds in 1898 leading to rapid settlement and major mining development, the area boomed. The richest mines in the early days were the Broad Arrow Consols, Hill End and the Golden Arrow. During the war years of 1914 to 1922, the major producers of gold were the Oversight and Tara leases. These two mines yielded 17 400 ounces of gold, a substantial quantity for the time.

The railway line from Kalgoorlie north to Menzies arrived in Broad Arrow in November 1897, just three months after its commencement. The line was completed to Menzies in March 1898. With water supply an ongoing problem for steam locomotives, five giant salt water condensers were built along the line to help alleviate the problem. The Broad Arrow Water Tower holds a 25 000 gallon cast iron water tank and is still used today by the town.

By the mid 1920s the rush to Broad Arrow was over and the town was then virtually abandoned.

YES! CREDIT GIVEN
TO ANY PERSON OVER THE AGE OF 87
WITH ASSETS EXCEEDING $100000 AND
ACCOMPANIED BY BOTH PARENTS...
CARLTON MID
VB
VICTORIA BITTER
CARLTON DRAUGHT
CARLTON MID
DOUBLE HOPPED
CARLTON

with Salad

Steak with lot 8.00

ham or corn beef 9.00

Salad 12.50

Extras: tomato, cheese 4.50

beetroot lettuce 6.00

tea or coffee 5.0

Coke

burg

burg

bac

Chic

C

Cameron Corner Store

Commercial Hotel

Conargo Hotel

Cuttabri Wine Shanty

Cameron Corner Store

Although this remote watering hole, which sits on the Queensland side of the border fence, is 'modern' by bush pub standards, it has already forged a reputation as a classic since opening in 1989.

Cameron Corner Store
Cameron Corner via Tibooburra
Queensland
(08) 8091 3872

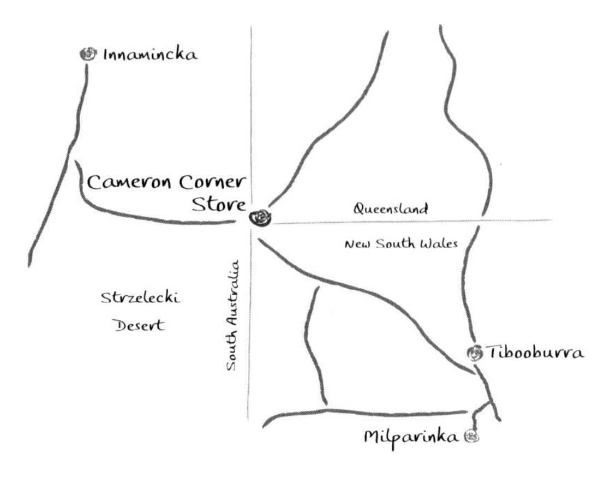

As far as outback bush pubs go, the Cameron Corner Store could quite easily be coined as the proverbial 'pub in the middle of nowhere!' It's 140 kilometres north-west from Tibooburra, its nearest neighbouring town of size. To add to the confusion, the 'Corner Store' is situated in Queensland, has a New South Wales postal address and rounds off with a South Australian telephone number!

Plonked right smack at the state border junctions of Queensland, New South Wales and South Australia, Cameron Corner is a popular destination for adventurous visitors exploring the corner country and is a popular stop for those travelling through from one state to the other.

It doesn't matter what time of the year you visit Cameron Corner Store, there's the likely chance that you'll meet workers from the oil and gas fields, shearers, truck drivers, doggers, gate keepers, farmers and shooters. There's generally someone about to have a yarn with. During the peak outback tourist season you are sure to come across a traveller or two stopping by for a drink or fuel and a chat about where they've been and where they're going. With such an eclectic group of customers you never know how your night at the Corner Store is going to pan out!

The Corner Store was built in 1989 by Sandy Nhall who spent two weeks at the Corner Post counting the number of visitors who stopped and then continued on. Sandy saw an opportunity and built the Corner Store. To date, there has only been two owners after Sandy.

TOYOTA
EXIT
MAGIC MILLIONS
OUTBACK AUSTRALIA
CAMERON CORNER
QLD. N.S.W. S.A.
EVERLAST
Bundaberg
Coca-Cola

Cameron Corner Store

The Surveyor's Saga

Cameron Corner bears the name of Scottish born surveyor John Cameron, who, along with Queensland surveyor George Watson, was employed by the NSW Lands Department to lead the first official survey party along the New South Wales-Queensland border between 1879 and 1881. This was along the 29th parallel south.

Starting the survey from the NSW town of Barringun after completing astronomical readings and building a 'zero' obelisk, Cameron and his party set out west towards the South Australian border on 2 September, 1879. Taking 12 months to complete the arduous task and hampered by searing heat, drought and flood, the party arrived (minus Watson who withdrew from the survey at the 100 mile post) at the intersection of the three states in September 1880. Cameron erected a wooden posted engraved 'Lat 29', along with the inscription 'Cameron'. The original wooden post, which is on display at the Tibooburra NPWS office, was replaced in June 1969 with a concrete pillar.

The party returned to Barringun and then started their survey to the east towards the MacIntyre River, finally completing the New South Wales-Queensland border survey in October 1881.

Of all the state border intersecting points on the Australian mainland, the most easily accessible is Cameron Corner – and its got a pub!

MITCHELL

BILL'S CORNER
HOLE IN THE WALL

Commercial Hotel

The Commercial Hotel is a classic pub. Here, what you see is what you get and you'll find there is no pretence of it being anything other than a small town country hotel.

Commercial Hotel
Dowling Street, Bendoc
Victoria
(02) 6458 1453

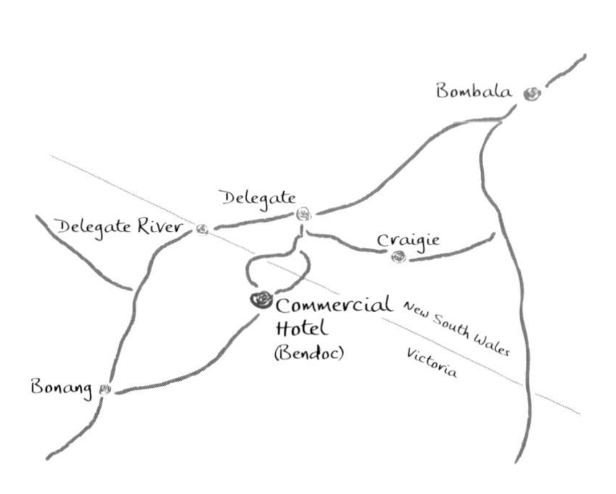

Bendoc is a small timber town located in Victoria's far East Gippsland, just south of the New South Wales border.

The town's only drinking hole, the Commercial Hotel was first licenced in 1888, but originally stood opposite its current location. Half of the original building was burnt in a fire, and the remains of the other half are still standing opposite the hotel.

Not surprisingly, being in a timber town, the Commercial is built from local timber of rough sawn weatherboards, with internal architraves and door frames cut from wattle.

Once through the front door off the wide verandah there is the small front bar and a lounge area with a roaring fire in the winter. Behind the bar is the pool table.

Typical of many Victorian hotels, pots of beer are served in dimpled handled glasses.

Bendoc isn't on the well-worn tourist route, so you'll more than likely meet one of the few locals at the bar. Once you get this lot chatting there is no stopping them! They may even let you in on where the monster trout which adorn the walls were caught.

Bendoc's beginnings stem from an 1866 gold rush, and grew with the timber industry. West of town is the Delegate River Tunnel, a small tunnel hacked through solid rock by Chinese miners, and to the south of town are the verdant forests of the Errinundra Plateau, the scene of a violent protest between loggers and conservationists in the 1980s. It is now a national park.

in the dark!
TOM QUILTY
GOLD CUP
100 MILER
CUSTOMS WATCH
1800 06 1800
Vineyard
BAR

COMMERCIAL HOTEL
BENDOC
M
MELBOURNE
BITTER

HANDS OFF
CARLTON DRAUGHT

COMMERCIAL HOTEL
BENDOC
M
MELBOURNE
BITTER

Conargo Hotel

Thirty five kilometres north-east of Deniliquin on the back road to Jerilderie, Conargo Hotel's icon status is partly due to the ubiquitous black and white bumper sticker seen on utes the country over.

Conargo Hotel
McKenzie Street, Conargo
New South Wales
(03) 5884 6607

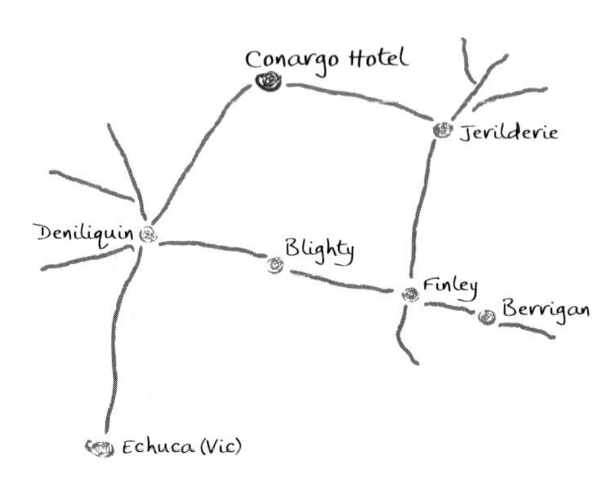

The Conargo Hotel was completed in 1853 as one of three pubs in the Conargo township. Located along the Cobb & Co Jerilderie to Deniliquin route, there is an old drop log stable just down the road a bit from the pub.

Conargo is renown for sheep stud breeding. The Peppin family developed the Peppin Merino bloodline during the 1860s which still plays a major role in the region's prestigious breeding. Photos, awards and newspaper articles of the area's sheep breeding heritage adorn the inside walls of the hotel.

Carrying the sheep grazing theme through the pub is the amenities block out the back that has been made of recycled shearing shed materials dating from around 1912.

Another fine feature of the hotel is the bar which is made from a single piece of oregon salvaged from an old flour mill.

Along with sheep, the region also farms cereal crops and you'd be hard pressed not to find one of the local cockies in the pub talking about the current weather, grain or wool prices. We've even heard bragging rights to who got the most rain in their gauge out of the last shower!

Stories of the mythical bunyip abound out here. Some believed that these were seals that had made their way from the ocean up river to live in the river's billabongs and lagoons. Legend has it that for a time there was a stuffed bunyip, which had been shot in a nearby lagoon in about 1870, on the mantlepiece of the Conargo Hotel

CONARGO PUB
CONARGO PUB
UTE MUSTER

Conargo EST 1853 Hotel
Specials
Specials

Beaut Utes

One of the most enduring symbols of the 'bush' is the ute. The celebration of ute culture is alive and well in the Riverina, and no more so when utility afficionados come together on the New South Wales Labour Day Long Weekend for the Deni Ute Muster. The muster kicked off after a group of Deniliquin locals decided to start a rural festival to bring tourists to the region.

The first muster was held in October 1999 and the parade of 2,839 legally registered utes made it into the Guinness Book of Records. Since then the festival and muster have become one of the most important weekends on the Friggers (an unusual term used for a young ute loving person) calendar, with the number of utes continuing to grow annually.

In 2008 the record was broken again with 7,242 utes on parade, along with the Blue Singlet count of 2,702 – that's people wearing a blue singlet!

When it comes to show time there's all models, makes, sizes, shapes, modifications – basically anything goes when it comes to the utes on display at the ute muster.

Come October's Ute Muster in nearby Deniliquin, the pub really starts jump'n when up to 500 revellers converge on the place.

Cuttabri Wine Shanty

Quaint: oddly picturesque; having an old-fashioned attractiveness or charm. That's the Cuttabri Wine Shanty, a hidden treasure tucked away along a back road on the northern side of the Pilliga Scrub.

Cuttabri Wine Shanty
Pilliga Road, Cuttabri
New South Wales
(02) 6796 2240

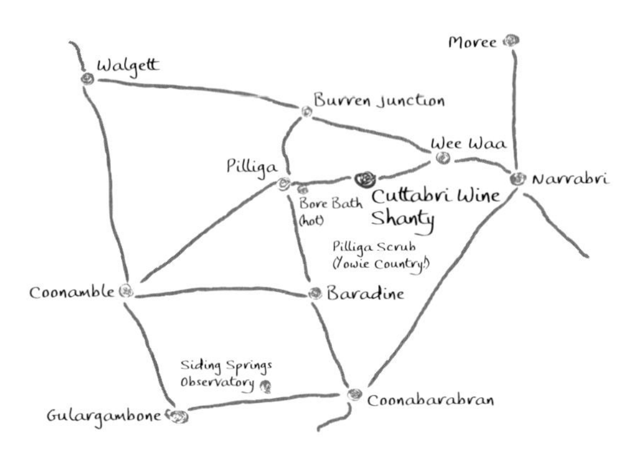

The Cuttabri Wine Shanty was built in 1883 by William and Elizabeth Trindall and originally named the 'Bee Hive'. It is believed to have been issued with the second liquor licence in Australia.

The Bee Hive was a 20-room hotel made from local pine and ironbark slabs and roofed with shingles. In 1900 the Bee Hive burnt down and tragically Elizabeth died from burns she sustained from the fire whilst trying to save the furniture. One piece of furniture that survived the fire is a cabinet that was hand-carved by Elizabeth. This still stands proudly in the corner of The Shanty's dining room.

A new hotel was built by James and Elizabeth Hall on the same site of the Bee Hive, the Halls took over the licence after the fire, naming it the Cuttabri Wine Shanty and opened for business in 1903. During these times Cuttabri was a busy community, being a stopover for Cobb & Co coaches, travellers, sleeper cutters and teamsters.

With the coming of the railway, which bypassed Cuttabri, the community declined to all but the Shanty, which continued to trade.

Since its opening in 1883 there have been only six licensees of the Cuttabri Wine Shanty.

Inside the weatherboard and timber building is a cosy front bar. The bar, although small, is packed with character. In fact, you'll probably find a local character or two warming themselves by the fire.

In addition to the front bar there is another welcoming room with a pool table and out back is an attractive dining room. Adorning the walls of

125
10th MAY
CAMPING
TOILETS
WOOD CHOP
NEW

these rooms is an eclectic display of memorabilia and antiques from the area.

Out front the verandah is bathed in sunlight in the late afternoon, making it an inviting place to relax. The pub dog and cat can often be found doing exactly that. When it's cold, the firepits, made from old plough discs, provide a focal point to chat by out on the front lawn.

Located to the south of Cuttabri, The Pilliga Scrub is reputed to be a favoured haunt for yowies; ape like creatures of Aboriginal mythology and Australian folklore. In mid 1999 a group of yowie hunters staged an expedition to the Pilliga Forests with the hope of seeking out these rarely seen but often talked about beasts. Claims of an unknown creature rustling in the undergrowth was cause for great excitement for these intrepid researchers. However photographic evidence of the creature's existence failed to eventuate. Once again the Pilliga yowie had managed to avoid detection, throwing wide open the age old debate as to whether the yowie is fact or fiction. We asked a few of the locals at the Shanty about the Pilliga yowies, but were told not to worry, as 'we've eaten them all'.

Not keen on a glass of plonk? Then there's no need to worry, The Shanty was granted a licence to sell beer some years ago.

It began its life as a bark hut in the early 1880s and is now the only remaining operating wine shanty.

PILLIGA LANDS
FORGET THE DOG
BEWARE OF THE OWNER
Streets
HOUSE POLICY
FREE BEER
TOMORROW
No more. It's the Law.
XXXX
Beer

CARNIVAL
OF THE ANIMALS
YOUNG PERSON'S
GUIDE to the
ORCHESTRA
COLUMBIA
PRIVATE

Carson Ltd.
Beer is proof that
God loves us and
wants us to be happy.
HOT IN THE CITY
TONIGHT
Shell
JIM BEAM
PROFESSIONAL JD DRINKER
IN TRAINING
JACK DANIEL'S
Tennessee
WHISKEY
Old
No.7
PRIVATE

HAHN
Premium Light
PREMIUM LAGER
TOOHEYS
EXTRA DRY
1958
NT
DRAUGHT
BEER

Daly Waters Pub

Dargo Hotel

Daly Waters Pub

On any night this little outback pub can be packed to the rafters with travellers from all over the world, but it once was the haunt of drovers, flying mailmen and military personnel.

Daly Waters Pub
Main Street, Daly Waters
Northern Territory
(08) 8975 9927

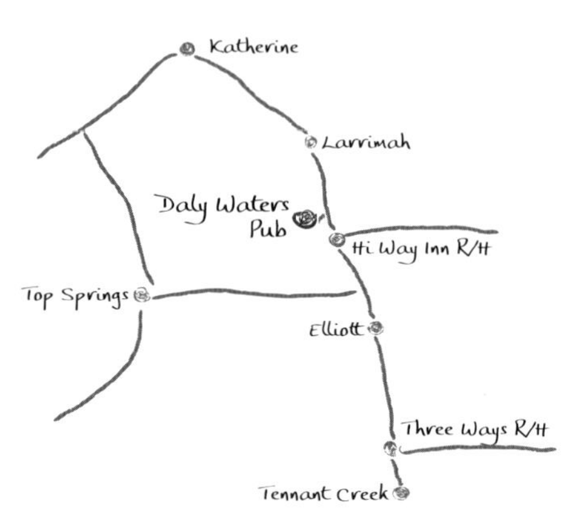

Explorer John McDouall Stuart named Daly Waters in 1862. Stuart was passing through the area on his third attempt to cross the Australian continent from south to north, and after having spent weeks cutting through almost impenetrable lancewood scrub he stumbled across a waterhole, where he and his party rested before continuing north.

Ten years later, in August 1872, the Overland Telegraph Line was completed and joined at Frews Ponds, south of Daly Waters. By 1887 a staff of five were located at the Telegraph Station.

In 1928 Bill and Henriette Pearce and their daughter Elizabeth settled at Daly Waters where they built a store to provide a service to travellers along the long, lonely stretch of road. The store then became the pub towards the end of the 1930s.

In 1930 an airfield was built to service the mail plane on its run between Daly Waters, Birdum and further destinations.

With the outbreak of World War II, the Daly Waters airfield was upgraded to become a base for both Australian and American bomber and fighter squadrons, flying bombing missions to PNG.

After the war Daly Waters' airfield was commissioned as Australia's first international airport, acting as a dispersal point for airmail to the United Kingdom as well as a re-fuelling strip for international passenger aircraft.

DALY WATERS PUB
1930
XXXX
Coca-Cola
Coke
BEEF
BARRA
Book at the
BAR

CATWALK
DALY WATERS
HISTORIC
PUB
THE CHILDRENS CHARITY
REECEPSHUN
LAST
PUB
Castrol

The Pearce's supplied meals for the airline staff and to the growing number of passengers, and were renowned for their friendly service and unique bush hospitality.

When the war drew to a close, Daly Waters swiftly declined to a small community made up of aerodrome staff and local farmers. The Pearce's left the pub around this time, and in 1971 the aerodrome was officially closed.

Throughout all this the Daly Waters Pub managed to survive, and is still a popular watering hole for travellers from across Australia and around the world.

Although Daly Waters is a 'tourist' pub, it still hasn't lost its character appeal, and unlike a lot of the Territory's hotels, which are basically roadhouses with a bar, Daly Waters is essentially a bush pub. There's plenty of mementos from past visitors and memorabilia lining the walls.

During the dry season the pub offers up its nightly Beef & Barra dinner which is especially popular with the grey nomad set. Dished up in the outdoor barbecue area, travellers come far and wide to experience this unique Daly Waters phenomenon.

Many pub visitors have left their mark in the form of flags, currency, ID cards and anything else they might have been carrying on their journey.

FOR 27-08-2006
AM NEXT YEAR.
BEERANDBULLSHITCORNER
Pauls
ATM
STREETS

NT Draught
YARCK HOTEL
HIRE & SALES
2009
12
2

Dargo Hotel

High up in Victoria's alpine country, Dargo sits in a picturesque valley and has been a favoured stopping place for fortune-seeking goldminers, mountain cattlemen and travellers since the 1860s.

Dargo Hotel
Lind Avenue, Dargo
Victoria
(03) 5140 1231

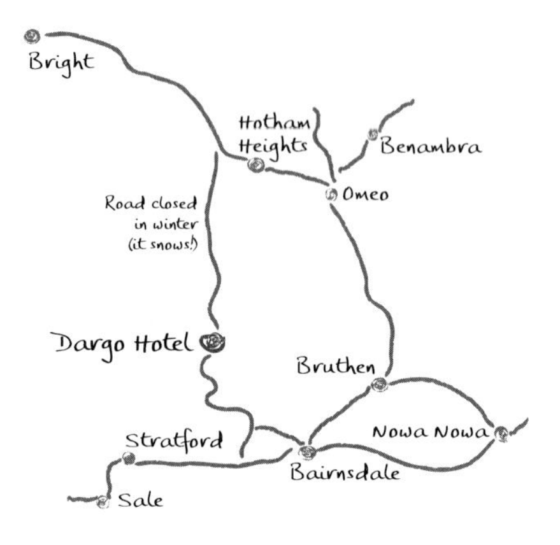

Dargo grew into a major stopover point in the 1860s when miners would stop at the village for fresh supplies and a night at the pub before heading to the uncertainty of the goldfields. There were a number of drinking establishments operating in Dargo at that time and it is said that intoxicated prospectors would often stagger out of the hotels into Dargo's cold night air, only to be found the next morning with beards frozen solidly into the puddles in which they had fallen!

Patrick Coloe established a new hotel at Dargo in 1881. Centrally located opposite the courthouse, The Bridge Hotel supposedly soon became a popular venue and offered good accommodation.

By 1896 The Bridge Hotel was the town's only remaining licenced hotel, but in March 1899 the hotel was destroyed by fire, and rebuilt from demolished buildings from the deserted gold township of Grant.

The Bridge Hotel was taken over by Dan Hurley in 1913 and the hotel remained within the Hurley family for almost 70 years. In the mid 1980s the hotel changed its name to the Dargo Hotel.

Apparently the old timers weren't too happy when electricity came to town, the newfangled way of serving the beer cold from a temprite, as opposed to cellar temperature, offered up a jar of ale far too cold for them!

A great example of a high country hotel, the timber and iron building is surrounded by a large verandah on two sides. Inside there is a front bar with a large dining room off to one side.

CARLTON
DARGO HOTEL
BAR & BISTRO
5140 1251
SINGLETS $22.00
POLO SHIRTS $35.00
DARGO CAPS & FISHING HATS $20.00
HORSE CENTRE
DARGO COMMUNITY BUS
$2.00
Intoxication
No Proof No Entry
No Proof No Purchase
Be Safe in Public Places
Penalty – $6,000
EXTRA COLD
Dargo School Fundraiser
DARGO HOTEL
DARGO HOTEL STICKERS $3.00
DARGO HOTEL
DARGO HOTEL STUBBIE HOLDERS $9.00
FUJI
NEXT 2000 km
CARLTON DRAUGHT
CARLTON DRAUGHT

Coopers

G

Gladstone Hotel

Glengarry Hilton

Grand Hotel

Grove Hill Hotel

Gladstone Hotel

Wyandra's second pub was built in 1889 and named the Gladstone. After burning to the ground in 1927, the hotel was rebuilt and is still pretty much the same today as when it reopened in 1929.

Gladstone Hotel
Railway Street, Wyandra
Queensland
(07) 4654 0273

The Gladstone Hotel is the only remaining hotel in Wyandra, and not much has changed at the single storey, timber and corrugated iron building.

The interior of the Gladstone Hotel is clean and sparse. There are no bras, undies, hats or t-shirts hanging from the ceiling; the walls are devoid of scribbles, business cards and overseas licences; there are no pin boards of photographs of partying backpackers – Wyandra is a little too far off the well-worn tourist route for this caper. It's a pleasant change for a bush pub.

Walking in off the street beneath the wide shady verandah you enter the main bar room. The bar – long by bush pub standards – wraps around in an L shape, and the hotel's original cellar is still below it. Above the bar hang framed pictures of racehorses crossing the finishing line at local race meetings. The separate dining room is bright and cheery with laminate tabletops and brightly coloured chairs and curtains.

Wyandra sits on the banks of the Warrego River, north of Cunnamulla and was a Cobb & Co stop on the Cunnamulla to Charleville run.

The railway from Charleville reached town in 1897 and in the following year it was extended to Cunnamulla. These were the heady days of Wyandra; with the railway came passenger, freight and mail transport, as well as a rail ambulance.

After the introduction of road freight the railway wasn't used as extensively as it once was and with its closure saw a decline in the town's prosperity.

About sixty people now live in Wyandra.

GLADSTONE HOTEL
WYANDRA
XXXX Our beer. XXXX
Wins on
Every time.
VICTORIA BITTER
CARLTON MID
XXXX GOLD LAGER
OPEN

Glengarry Hilton

The sign says 'Welcome to the World Famous Glengarry Hilton'. We're not sure who's world it's famous in, but the Glengarry is nothing like any other Hilton you'll have visited!

Glengarry Hilton
Glengarry Opal Fields
New South Wales
(02) 6829 3808

Situated within the heart of the Glengarry Opal Fields, the Glengarry Hilton is a popular oasis with opal gougers who relax under the shady breezeway between the bar and main building. The pub's a huge ramshackle space set-off with a rustic collection of handmade timber furniture.

The bar resembles a corrugated iron garden shed, the likes you'd find in the average suburban backyard, while the main part of the pub houses a pool table, dining area and a couple of slow combustion wood heaters for those chilly midwinter opal field nights.

Surrounded by a parched landscape, it'll come as no suprise that at day's end you'll come across someone enjoying a couple of 'quite ones' at the Glengarry Hilton. There's a carved sign on the pub's door which reads: 'Trading Hours 6am to 6am 8 days a week CLOSED NEVER'.

This is a bush pub with stacks of character and there's a lot of human characters there too.

The Glengarry and neighbouring Grawin opal fields are an interesting destination to the west of Lightning Ridge and north-west of Walgett. The road into the Glengarry Hilton snakes its way past open mine shafts – the fields littered with mullock heaps and assorted mining machinery made from disused cars, trucks or any other types of mechanical item that could be utilised. Some of the residents live in small tin huts, while others boast more elaborate abodes, some even sporting well maintained flower gardens!

VIETNAM VETERAN
Seafood
TRAY
RAFFLES
SWEENEYS
ART · CRAFTS
LIKE TO HAVE A
LOOK!
ASK AT THE BAR
GLADIATORS MC GUNNEDAH
CHRISTMAS
DINNER
Christmas Eve
Buffet
NEW YEAR'S
EVE PARTY
Live ENTERTAINMENT
Good Food / Free Keg

WELCOME TO THE...
'WORLD FAMOUS'
GLENGARRY HILTON
GLENGARRY HILTON

COUGAR
XXXX GOLD
TOOHEYS NEW
SMOOTH
EASY DRINKING
DRAUGHT BEER

CHRISTMAS DINNER
$12 pp
Christmas Eve
Buffet Please Book
NEW YEAR'S EVE PARTY
Live ENTERTAINMENT
Good Food / Free Keg.

GLENGARRY HILTON
Friendly Service
ICE COLD BEER & DRINKS
HOT & COLD MEALS
ACCOMMODATION

Grand Hotel

The real estate adage of 'Location, location, location' was the saving grace for the Grand Hotel at Kookynie. As the town's other six hotels ceased trading one by one, the Grand lived on!

Grand Hotel
Britannia Street, Kookynie
Western Australia
(08) 9031 3010

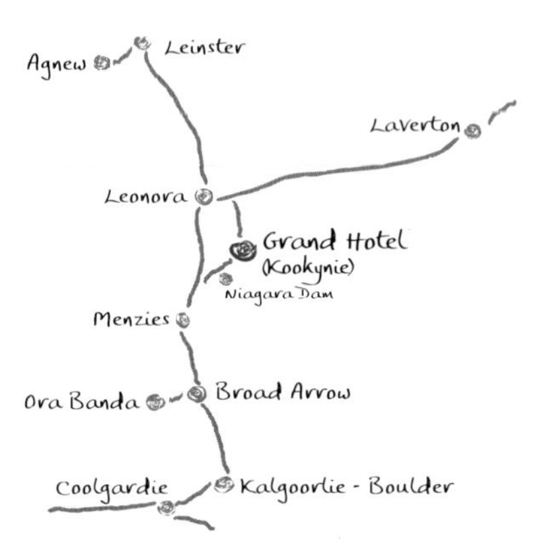

Trading since November 1902, the Grand Hotel was described at the time as not one of the 'grandest' hotels in town. Today, though, the Grand Hotel evokes a grandeur of its own in the once prosperous mining town. Internally it has fabulously high ceilings, large hallways, wide doorways and pressed metal ceilings with ceiling roses. On the walls of the main hallway hangs a collection of framed history, pictures and maps along with an assortment of rusty old tools from a bygone era.

Whilst patronage of the other six licenced hotels in the town slowly declined after the declaration of the Great War, the Grand Hotel managed to survive, most likely due to its location being directly opposite the railway station. This hotel, unlike the others, was the first and last stopping point in town for all those travelling by train, four of which arrived daily from Kalgoorlie.

In its heyday Kookynie was a town with 400 buildings and a resident population of around 3,500, with a similar number of transients. The town even boasted its own swimming baths and a booming red light district run by Japanese ladies.

Of the 400 buildings in Kookynie, there were seven licenced hotels and four private hotels. At the time private hotels were only permitted to serve alcohol to their house guests. However, house guests were also allowed to invite along seven of their own guests. Luckily, the town had its own brewery, so the pubs never ran dry.

GRAND HOTEL
KOOKYNIE

EMU
EXPORT
LAGER
The Right Stuff!
Save Your Local.
LOCAL BUTCHER
LOCAL BAKER
LOCAL BANK
LOCAL HOTEL
VICKS
VapoDrops
Allen's

The Beginning of the End

Kookynie was born from gold with the first leases taken up in 1895. In 1897 one of these leases was purchased by the London-owned Cosmopolitan Proprietary Ltd. The Cosmopolitan was to extract the largest amount of gold from the area, however its demise came in 1910 when the company halted operations due to constant flooding of the mine. Generally not an issue for most gold mining regions, on the Kookynie leases underground artesian reservoirs proved problematic. The underground waters were pumped to the surface and then channelled away. Sometimes the excess waters overflowed, ending up in the town's streets causing minor flooding. The cost to constantly run the pumps day and night eventually made the mine unviable and the Cosmopolitan Mine ceased operations.

The ruins of two of the town's other hotels, The Cosmopolitan and The National are only a short stroll from the Grand. The National was said to have been 'elegant with comfort', which compared most favourably to 'similar establishments in the larger centres of population'.

At the end of World War I, as the town's population dwindled most of the buildings were dismantled, with materials recycled or buildings relocated to other areas.

All of Kookynie's seven hotels, bar the Grand Hotel, ceased to trade around 1911 when the ore ran out and the mines closed.

Grove Hill Hotel

Tucked away beside a section of the 'old' Stuart Highway to the north of Pine Creek, the heritage listed Grove Hill Hotel is a living example of a 1930s depression era pub.

Grove Hill Hotel
Mt Wells Road, Grove Hill
Northern Territory
(08) 8978 2489

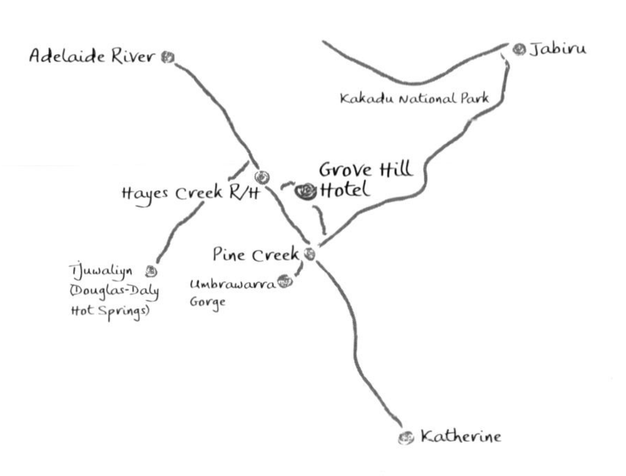

Constructed of whatever was lying about at the time, Grove Hill Hotel shows the ingenuity of recycling, long before recycling became trendy. Built during the economic downturn between the wars, when money and building materials were scarce, much of the hotel comprises items scavenged from nearby gold mines and tramways. The pub is on the Northern Territory Heritage Register and the Register of the National Estate.

The hotel building, although a hotchpotch of timber, steel and corrugated iron, certainly has a unique charm. This strangely fascinating structure just draws you in. Inside it is surprisingly cool with its concrete floors and louvred windows, and there's a museum with a treasure-trove of historic memorabilia for visitors to explore.

Prospector and master blacksmith Bill Lucy, along with his wife Margaret, built the Grove Hill Hotel between 1933 and 1936. The Lucys were evacuated during World War II but returned to the pub after the war. Bill died in the 1950s, but the incorrigible Margaret continued running the hotel until she fell ill and retired in 1972.

The hotel was closed for nearly 20 years until Jan Hills and Pip Bremner purchased the run-down property in 1990, undertaking sympathetic renovations. In 1993 the pub recommenced trading, and has been ever since.

To date there have only been three licensees of the Grove Hill Hotel; the Lucys, Jan Hills and the current licensees, the Haeuslers.

A DRINKING PROBLEM
ENAGERS
TIRED OF BEING HARASSED BY YOUR STUPID PARENTS
ACT NOW!!!!!
BEWARE of the OWNER
This House Guarded by
SHOTGUN
3 Nights per Week
BALD IS BEAUTIFUL
GOD MADE ALL HEADS BALD
Dear Lord.....
Nobody is Perfect
WYBMADIITY
ACCOMMODATION PER NIGHT
BAR-B-Q
CAMPING
CARAVAN SITE
POWER EXTRA
MUSIC
BAR RULES
FOUREX
XXXX
BEER O'CLOCK
CARLTON
GOLD

PLEASE
DONT
TOUCH

BAR
CARLTON

XXXX
GOLD

Grove Hill
Historic Hotel 16

GROVE HILL
GROVE HILL HERITAGE
CANS
Coca-Cola
NO DOGS ALONG FENCE
WHISKEY

GROVE HILL HERITAGE

know
to grow them – to ma
TOOHEYS
DRAUGHT
GULF
LAGER
CAT Diesel Power
BEN
McANDREW
JOHNNIE WALKER
Red Label
KENTUCKY STRAIGHT
BOURBON WHISKEY
JAMES B BEAM DISTILLING CO
Bundaberg
Bundaberg

HEBEL HOTEL

HOMEBUSH HOTEL

Hebel Hotel

There's been a hotel at the border crossing settlement of Hebel since 1894. More than 100 years on the pub still offers up to travellers, stockmen and shearers a cleansing ale or two in the hotel's bar.

Hebel Hotel
William Street, Hebel
Queensland
(07) 4625 0923

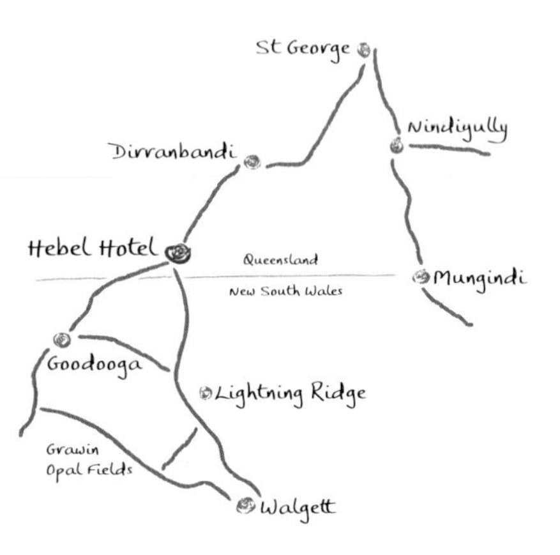

One of the great things about the Hebel Hotel is that it looks like it's always been there, sitting quietly beside the road serving passing travellers as it has done for well over a century. It's built in typical western Queensland style; weatherboard clad walls with a corrugated iron roof and a shady verandah out front.

In 1894 the Hebel Hotel officially opened as a Cobb & Co changing station, later commencing operations as a hotel. Still standing outside the pub are a number of rickety old posts which are the original horse hitching rails.

Inside, the pub consists of a front bar, with both the walls and ceiling clad with lining boards. There's a collection of shearing memorabilia with hand shears, wool bale bags, bale hooks, combs and station brands on the walls. Shearers still stop by the hotel for a couple of 'brown lemonades' after cut-out. The front verandah is a popular spot for the locals, especially in the afternoons and on those warm western downs evenings, to sit and spin a few yarns.

The 'blink and you'll miss it' settlement of Hebel is located just north of the New South Wales/Queensland border on the Castlereagh Highway, about midway between the towns of Walgett and St George.

Established in 1889 as a customs post, the burgeoning settlement was originally given the name Kelly's Point, allegedly after bushranger Dan Kelly, who is said to have resided in the area for a time, but this story seems highly unlikely.

HEBEL HOTEL
HEBEL HOTEL
CUSTOMERS
FIGHTS WILL NOT
BE TOLERATED
TIE UP YOUR
DOGS
THANKYOU

JIMAC
GRAZCOS

PUBLIC
BAH

XXXX Hebel Hotel XXXX

Apparently the town's name was changed to Hebel in the early 1890s after a German family that lived in town.

Back in the days before 'Tidy Town Awards' were in vogue, Hebel had the dubious distinction of hosting one of the largest bottle dumps in the country. Popular folklore has it that from the mid 1940s up until it was bulldozed in the mid 1960s, the collection of empty beer and rum bottles beside the pub measured 36 feet long by 21 feet wide. This pile of glass could be clearly seen from 30 000 feet above by planes en route from Sydney to Hong Kong – they used it as a navigation aid!

Along with bushrangers, and others of a less sinister nature, Lightning Ridge based artist John Murray has also left his mark on the Hebel Hotel with his quirky paintings. His work has enhanced the look and feel of this great little pub, giving it a uniqueness.

You'll find John's photo-realistic art is scattered throughout the hotel, on the exterior walls and doors, those fake front windows and obviously on the roof. And those whimsical animals, well, they have their own individual personalities and charm – just like the drinkers breasting the bar at the hotel.

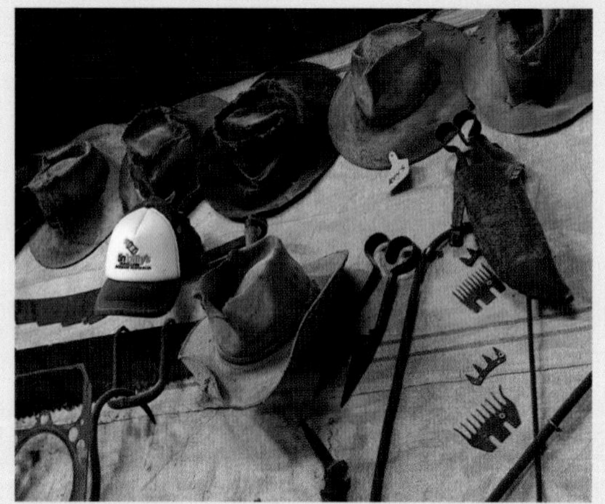

The Hebel Hotel is one of those bush pubs you simply can't drive past without wanting to call in, no matter what time of day!

15ml
15ml
15ml
15ml
variety
Sprite
NOBBYS
PEANUTS
VB
VICTORIA
BITTER
CASTLEMAINE
XXXX
BITTER
VICTORIA
VB
BITTER
Every Family Need

Homebush Hotel

The route between Balranald and Ivanhoe was once dotted with roadside inns, but today the Homebush Hotel is the only surviving watering hole for travellers along this long, lonely stretch of road.

Homebush Hotel
Ivanhoe Road, Penarie
New South Wales
(03) 5020 6803

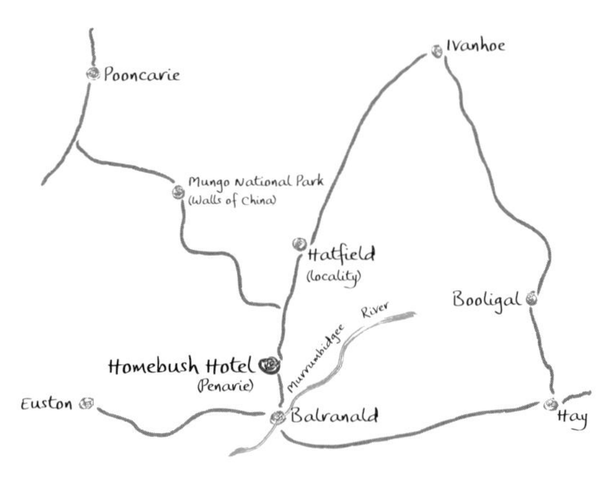

'G'day. Welcome to the Homebush' was the publican's greeting as we walked through the front door of the picturesque little pub at Penarie, about 27 kilometres north of Balranald on the road to Ivanhoe. The hotel stands sentinel over a vast, open plain, with little else surrounding it besides a few trees here and there to break the mirage. We instantly liked the place.

The external facade of the hotel hides a jumbled display of ornaments and other odds and ends. The front bar, together with a dining area and pool table is housed inside a large room with a centrally located fireplace. Off this main room are another two rooms which are chock-a-block full of antiques and assorted paraphernalia. But the front bar is the pub's focal point.

The Homebush Hotel is well patronised with people from all walks of life stopping by for a coldie. On any given day you'll come across shearers, farmers, truck drivers, timber cutters, travellers and even charcoal burners holding court at the bar. The pub's also becoming an increasingly popular stopover for visitors to and from the nearby World Heritage Listed Mungo National Park.

In September 1860 the Burke and Wills expedition passed to the west of where the hotel now stands on their way to Menindee after crossing the Murrumbidgee River at Balranald. They noted that there was already significant settlement occuring in the area.

Homebush Hotel commenced business in 1878 and has been dishing out its unique brand

1878
HOMEBUSH HOTEL

of outback hospitality ever since. Hanging on one of the inside walls is an honour board listing the hotel's numerous publicans, commencing with Michael Dowdican, the Homebush's foundation inn keeper. Dowdican originally owned the land on which the pub was built, located at the junction of the Balranald, Ivanhoe and Oxley roads. Dowdican's stay at the hotel lasted until 1896 when William Wilkinson became licensee.

During these early years of settlement pastoralists began pushing further west from the Riverina in search of grazing country. As the region become more settled, the route between Balranald and Ivanhoe transformed into a well-worn track, being regularly used to transport sizable wool clips by horse-drawn wagon to ports along the Murray River. It was also trafficked by prospectors heading to the western goldfields.

Roadside inns and hotels were built to serve the passing trade. A popular custom at the time was to plant a pepper tree out the front of these lonely roadside establishments. These days, a lone pepper tree silhouetted against the backdrop of a simmering saltbush plain represents the one time existence of a long gone hotel.

Michael Dowdican purchased land at the Balranald-Ivanhoe-Oxley road junction and built the Homebush Hotel.

ESTD CASTLEMAINE PERKINS 1878
XXXX
GOLD
AUSTRALIAN LAGER
TRADITIONALLY BREWED FOR FULL FLAVOUR
30 CANS x375mL
3.5% ALC/VOL CONTAINS APPROX 1.0 STANDARD DRINKS PER CAN
9 310876 020257
2451

Innamincka Hotel

Ironclad Hotel

Innamincka Hotel

In 1886, only 25 years after explorers Burke and Wills perished on the banks of Cooper Creek for the want of sustenance, the first hotel at the settlement of Innamincka was established.

Innamincka Hotel
South Terrace, Innamincka
South Australia
(08) 8675 9901

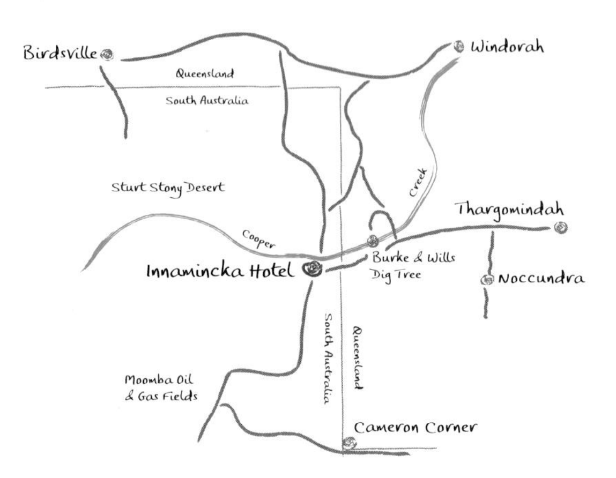

When the first hotel was set up on the banks of Cooper Creek in 1886, Innamincka was little more than a dusty outpost serving the hardy cattlemen who had started droving stock overland to the edge of the desert. The first European settlers were customs officers collecting taxes from droving parties crossing the border from Queensland.

The tiny settlement's pub operated in various guises until 1952 when the town itself virtually died. The pub then closed.

In the early 1970s the area experienced a surge in tourism and in 1973 a store was established. The hotel reopened with an accompanying motel which was re-named Cooper's Creek Hotel-Motel. In 1983, after the licence was suspended for a period, the hotel was again reopened and the name changed to Innamincka Hotel. This remote watering hole has seen many changes and renovations over the years and today's Innamincka Hotel is quite modern for an outback pub. Although the main bar area has changed little over the last lot of years, there is now a large dining room to cater for the seasonal influx of visitors – Sunday night dinners have always been a popular attraction.

Innamincka's remote location and connections with the Burke and Wills saga have made it a 'must visit' area on many people's travel itinerary. During the peak winter season the bar is likely to be frequented by travellers from all over Australia, plonked on one of the stools enjoying a drink.

And, after all our visits over the years, it's still a great spot to have a beer or two.

XXXX
GOLD
GOOD AS GOLD
ADL
741
73
SOUVENIRS
AKUBRA HERITAGE COLLECTION
WATERING HOLE
AKUBRA
GOLDEN ALE
NOW POURING

BURKE, WILLS & KING AT COOPER CREEK

A party of seven men from the Victorian Exploring Expedition arrived on the banks of Cooper Creek on November 20 1860, on their quest to be the first men to traverse the Australian continent from south to north.

After establishing a depot at Bulla Bulla Waterhole to the north of present day Innamincka, Burke, Wills, King and Gray set off in the oppressive summer heat, instructing the party left behind at Cooper Creek depot to return to Melbourne if they did not return within three months. They were to be presumed perished or having taken an alternative return route.

After four months and five days Burke, Wills and King returned to Cooper Creek on 21 April, 1861 to find that the depot was deserted – the depot party had departed only hours prior. A blazed tree with the same date advised of buried supplies.

After a continuation of mishaps, both Burke and Wills died some months later of starvation on the banks of the Cooper. John King was cared for by a group of Aborigines until his rescue by Alfred Howitt in September that year. He was the party's sole survivor.

Located east of the hotel is Burke's grave site and the Dig Tree while to the west is the grave site of Wills and King's marker.

Innamincka is remote, its nearest town being Tibooburra, some 340 odd kilometres to the south-east via Warri Warri Gate.

Coopers
INNAMINCKA
OTEL
BURKE
WILLS
ICE
• MOTEL ACCOMMODATION
• AIR CONDITIONED
• COLD BEER
CASTLEMAINE
XXXX
GOLD
LAGER

Ironclad Hotel

Marble Bar is listed in the Guinness Book of Records as being the hottest town in Australia. During late 1923 and early 1924, the town notched up 161 consecutive days over 38 degrees Celsius!

Ironclad Hotel
Francis Street, Marble Bar
Western Australia
(08) 9176 1066

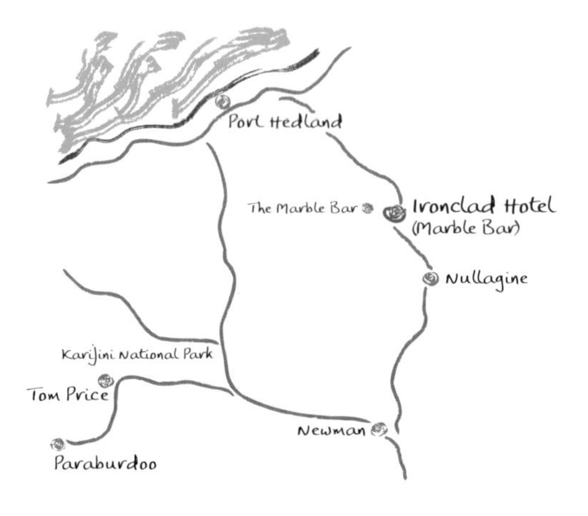

There is conjecture as to the origin of the name of Marble Bar's only remaining hotel, the Ironclad. Some sources suggest it was named after the richest mining claim in the area at the time, the Ironclad Lease, while others suggest a type of American boat – which operated on the Mississippi River at the time – provided inspiration, or was it simply named after the actual construction materials? It doesn't really matter either way, the Ironclad Hotel is just that, clad in iron. Even the pub's rustic interior has been given the corrugated and ripple iron treatment.

The Ironclad Hotel was built in 1892 at a time when there was an influx of prospectors to the East Pilbara goldfields. Originally, the Ironclad Hotel was one of two hotels in town; The Marble Bar Hotel which was opposite the Ironclad Hotel was de-licenced in 1915.

Except for a few renovations and additions over the years, the actual structure of the Ironclad Hotel hasn't changed much since it was first built. There are two bars, a back room with a pool table and a beer garden out the back with a small stage.

On the Coongan River, just five kilometres west of town is the colourful jasper stone bar which gold prospector Nathaniel Cook came across in the early 1880s. Cook, also a grazier, was looking for pasture for his drought affected sheep. Thinking the impressive jasper outcrop was marble, he named the area Marble Bar.

In 1888 alluvial gold was discovered on the Coongan River, beginning a rush to the area.

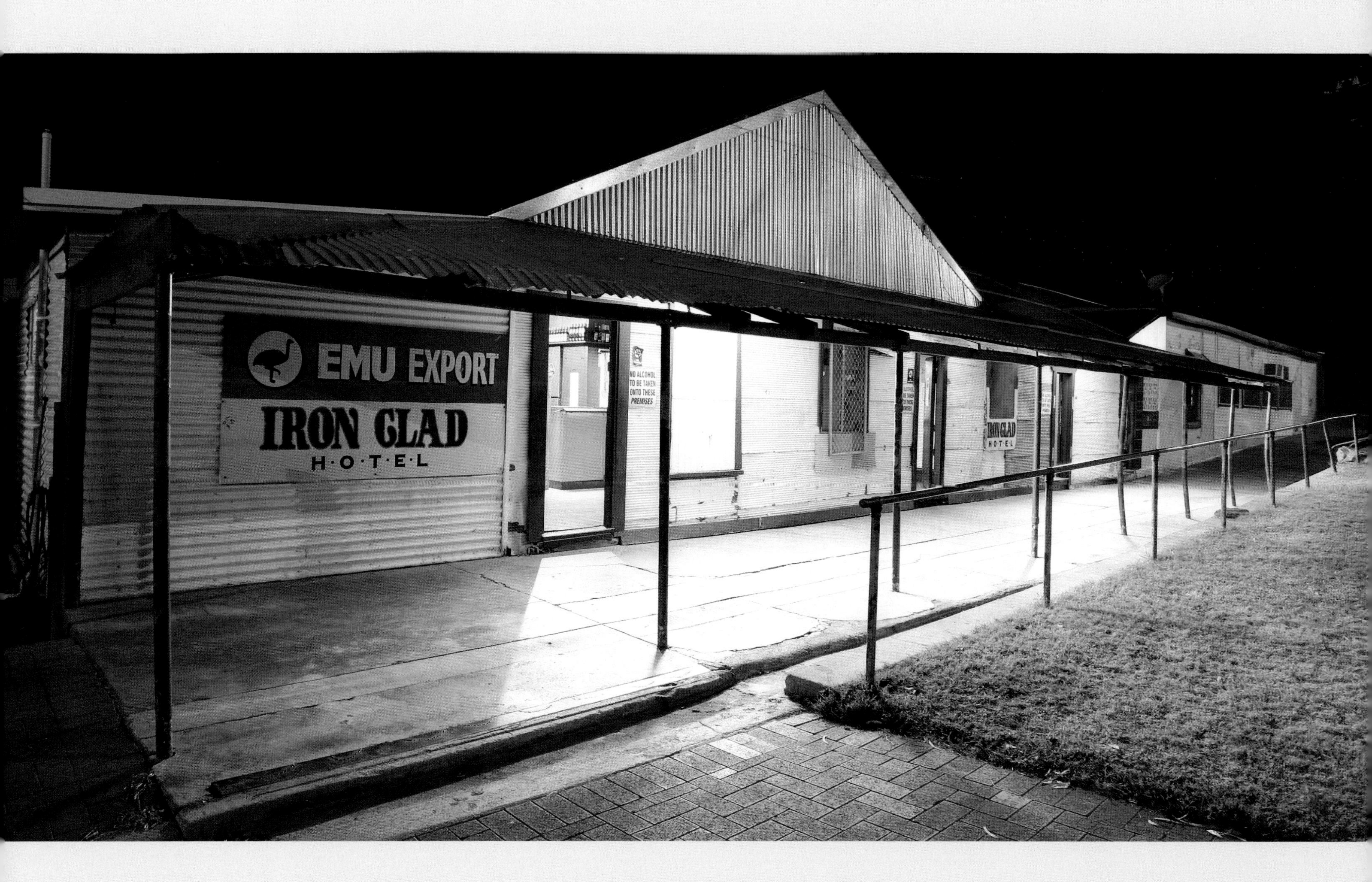
EMU EXPORT
IRON CLAD
H·O·T·E·L
NO ALCOHOL TO BE TAKEN ONTO THESE PREMISES
IRON CLAD
HOTEL

2 MILES TO F. JOHNSON & CO. GARAGE
CARLTON MID
EFTPOS IS HERE

NO SMOKING
18+
EMU
BITTER

EMU EXPORT
IRON CLAD
HOTEL

WARMEST WELCOME
FROM AUSTRALIAS
HOTTEST TOWN

EMU
DRAFT
MIDSTRENGTH
FULL FLAVOUR
VICTORIA
VB
BITTER

KINGOONYA PUB

Kingoonya Pub

Kingoonya Pub is one of those great outback institutions with a varied past. It has had its fair share of trials and tribulations and is now once again dispensing good old-fashioned hospitality in the bush.

Kingoonya Pub
Kingoonya Terrace, Kingoonya
South Australia
(08) 8672 1002

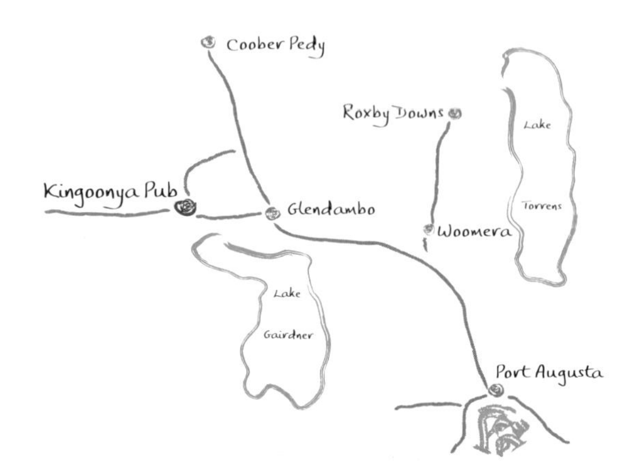

First opened in 1937 in what was then a thriving outback South Australian town, the Kingoonya Pub's prosperity was buoyed by passing trade along the Stuart Highway, the Trans-Continental Railway and helped by local graziers and shearers.

Interestingly, there were two applications to build and licence the town's first hotel. The 'favourite' with locals was Eileen Brett from Port Augusta, who was given the go ahead after a hearing was held in the bar of the town's racecourse. The hotel was built in a record six months!

Eileen Brett, later Crosby, ran the hotel along with her husband until her death in 1960. The lease was then transferred to Eileen's son Neill, who, along with his wife, stayed on at the pub until 1971.

Then, in the early 1980s when the Stuart Highway was re-routed to the east, the death knell sounded for Kingoonya after many of the townfolk had their houses transported to the new Glendambo Village. In 1982 when the hotel's licence expired it was transferred to the new hotel/roadhouse at Glendambo. The pub closed. Kingoonya became a ghost town.

The hotel fell into a state of disrepair and was ravaged by vandals until an Adelaide man, Paul Dryga, who was passing through town, reasoned the hotel building would make an ideal base from which to operate his long-term mineral drilling explorations in the area. Settlement covenants precluded Dryga from reopening the old Kingoonya Hotel as a licenced pub.

KINGOONYA
HOTEL
DONALD
86721002
DRAUGHT
Please Keep Off

WETSUIT
WATERING HOLE
LAST PUB FOR
240 Km
Daily MENU
ELKE MARGARET
KINGOONYA
HAHN
4:00
4:50
PURE BLONDE
KINGOONYA

In 1997, ten years after purchasing the building Dryga applied for and was granted a licence, after he reasoned that reopening the old pub at Kingoonya would pose no threat to the now well-establish Glendambo Hotel. In December 2003 the hotel recommenced business with a leasee, some 21 years after the call of 'last drinks'.

Dryga sold the pub in September 2005 to the Taylor family. They had long been passionate advocates of the hotel's history and remote outback location. After remaining closed for essential renovations, the pub reopened its doors in late 2006 and is again dispensing hospitality to travellers.

The pub still retains much of its charm. It's a substantial building constructed of concrete with a corrugated iron roof. There's a wide verandah around the front of the building – an ideal spot to relax as the sun sinks in the western sky. Trainspotters are kept happy with the Trans-Continental Railway running past the front of the pub.

Inside, the side verandah has been enclosed and now serves as the front bar and dining room while the original bar room now hosts a pool table.

These days Kingoonya has a permanent population of less than 10 people, so there's a good chance you'll meet one or two in the bar.

Kingoonya is reputed to have the widest main street in Australia, with cricket matches having been played on it!

CARLTON
LIGHT
XXXX
GOLD

L

Larrimah Hotel

Lions Den Hotel

Larrimah Hotel

At 181.04 metres above sea level to the top of the bar, The Larrimah Hotel boasts the 'highest' bar in the Northern Territory. That's just one of the quirky things about this unique Top End bush pub.

Larrimah Hotel
Mahony Street, Larrimah
Northern Territory
(08) 8975 9931

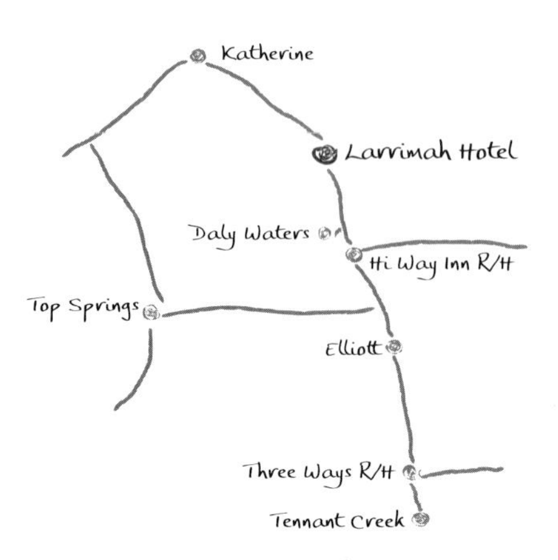

In the local Aboriginal Yangman language, Larrimah means 'meeting place', an apt word for this friendly little Top End hotel. Enveloped by shady trees and a huge verandah, it makes an ideal place to get together. Originally frequented by railway workers, truckies and drovers, the pub is now a firm favourite with tourists travelling along the Stuart Highway.

The Larrimah Hotel was partly constructed of materials recycled from the dismantled Birdum Hotel, which was located seven kilometres south of Larrimah. The building itself is a 'Sidney Williams' construction – a bolted steel frame construction clad in corrugated iron with wide eaves. This style of prefabricated building was popular during the war years as it enabled the building to be erected quickly and also easily dismantled so it could be moved to another location if required.

When the North Australia Railway was extended to Birdum, Catherine and Tim O'Shea, who had previously built hotels in remote parts of the Northern Territory, seized the opportunity to build a hotel at the new railhead. The pub, which was opened in 1929, soon became a well established drinking hole for drovers, train crews and passengers travelling the railway between Darwin and Birdum.

Birdum's days as a town were short-lived. The area's black soil caused the north-south road to become impassable during the wet season while the military – it was now wartime – saw that the bridge along this road was a possible target for

LARRIMAH HOTEL
Engine oil

enemy attack. These factors resulted in the railhead being moved north in 1941 to the site of present day Larrimah.

Larrimah soon became a military town. When Darwin was bombed in February 1942 by the Japanese, coastal shipping became a precarious proposition, necessitating the need for overland road and rail transport. Convoys of trucks from Alice Springs and Mt Isa streamed in and out of Larrimah, their cargoes transferred to rail for the final leg to Darwin.

By late 1945 Birdum was abandoned. The hotel was dismantled and moved, becoming the Larrimah Hotel, which opened in 1952.

Former publican Sidney Smith, a man well-versed in the ways of gaining media publicity, thought that a large pink panther – with fishing rod, sitting beside a puddle out the front of the pub – would make a good story. Smith proposed that Larrimah had the Northern Territory's smallest freshwater lake, and although it looked shallow it was in fact so deep that a road-train disappeared into it!

In 2003 the pub's future looked grim when an order to condemn the rambling old building was served. The foresight of a dedicated bunch of people saw the hotel saved from demolition. And it's still offering that renowned Top End hospitality today.

The pub is immediately recognisable from the highway thanks to the large NT stubby and pink panther sitting outside.

SNACKS
BREAKFAST
MAIN MEALS
TRADING HOURS
PLEASE BE PATIENT
BE REASONABLE DO IT MY WAY
BLOW JOB
MELBOURNE BITTER
Coopers
WE'RE AT LARRIMAH
THE HIGHEST BAR
NORTHERN TERRITORY
Peace Love Happiness

Lions Den Hotel

A north Queensland 'classic', the Lions Den Hotel is located south of Cooktown on the banks of the Little Annan River. Shaded by huge mango trees, the pub harks back to the days of old.

Lions Den Hotel
Shiptons Flat Road, Helenvale
Queensland
(07) 4060 3911

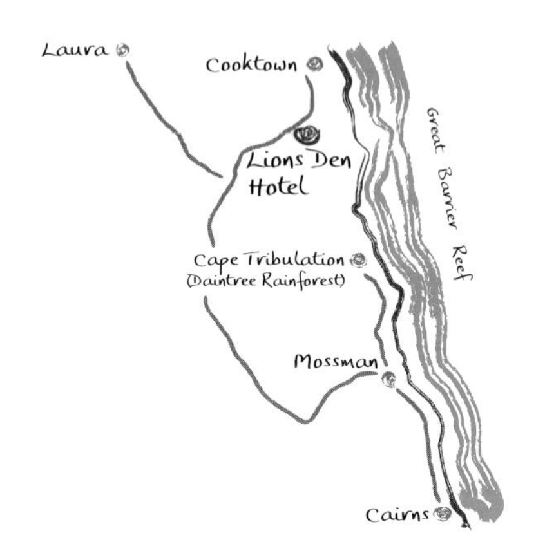

Built in 1875 out of bush poles and sawn timber and clad with corrugated iron inside and out, the Lions Den Hotel is set on the edge of lush north Queensland tropical rainforest. To the south is the famed World Heritage Listed Daintree Rainforest.

Popular legend has it that the pub took its name from a local tin mine, the Lions Den. Apparently the mine was nameless when a sailor by the name of Daniel, who had deserted his ship in Cooktown, showed up at the mine looking for work. The rookie employee, never having had to work underground before, was nicknamed 'Daniel in the Lions Den' by the mine's owner. From this came the mine's name as well as lending the moniker to the pub.

During the northern dry season, the Lions Den gets busy with travellers, especially with four-wheel drivers travelling the Bloomfield Track from Cape Tribulation north to Cooktown. It's also well patronised by the handful of locals and from the communities along the Bloomfield Track.

Outside there's a wide verandah fronting the pub, essential for those balmy tropical afternoons. Inside is a small front bar area along with a larger lounge bar cum dining area. The walls are plastered with countless names and signatures, along with a collection of anything and everything ranging from number plates, old bottles, hats, T-shirts and stubby holders. At the rear of the pub is a museum with a wonderful collection of old farm memorabilia and a natural history display of local snakes, fish, spiders and frogs.

B983 VJO
XXXX
XXXX BITTER
VICTORIA BITTER
VB
FOSTER'S
STRONGBOW
PIES
JERILDERIE HOTEL
support your local OUTLAWS
Coca-Cola
4WD
XXXX GOLD LAGER
VICTORIA

LIONS DEN
BROTHERS IN ARMS
XXXX
LIONS DEN
XXXX
XXXX
PLEASE!
NO TINNIES

CAIRNS DRAUGHT
SHOP
NOW
OPEN
THE NORTHS OWN BEER
Lager
GEORGE ST

EXIT

COOPERS BREWERY
Coopers
LAGER
PREMIUM
5.0% ALC/VOL

M

Marree Hotel

Middleton Hotel

Marree Hotel

Marree was once an important railway town as well as a base for the famous Afghan camel drivers who carried supplies to the outlying centres such as Oodnadatta, Birdsville and Alice Springs.

Marree Hotel

Railway Terrace, Marree

South Australia

(08) 8675 8344

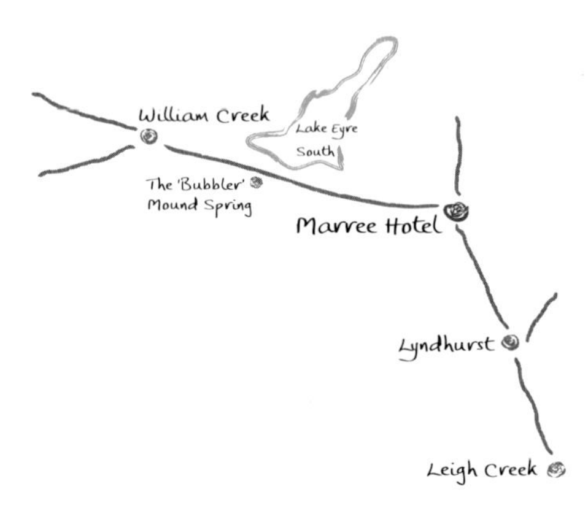

Early records show that this impressive sandstone building was 83 feet by 46 feet with a bar room of 19 feet by 22 feet and a dining room of 17 feet. It would have been quite an impressive public house in little more than a shanty settlement fringing the edge of the desert!

Located directly opposite the old railway station, The Great Northern Hotel, as it was originally known, was built to provide food and lodgings for travellers undertaking the once perilous railway journey on the Old Ghan and drovers moving cattle along the infamous Birdsville Track.

Hergott Springs was the original name given to the area after David Herrgott, a German botanist, who discovered the artesian springs nearby in 1859 whilst on an expedition with explorer John McDouall Stuart. In 1918, with anti-German sentiments having been rife during World War I, the name was officially changed to Marree.

In February 1884 the Central Australian Railway from Port Augusta was extended to Marree. This strategically positioned railhead then allowed for livestock from northern Queensland to be brought down the Birdsville Track and then transported to the Adelaide markets by rail. It wasn't long before the town's population boasted some 600 people along with numerous businesses.

In the early 1920s, when droving was in full swing, it wasn't uncommon for up to 20 000 mixed head of both sheep and cattle to be brought down the Birdsville Track each season 'on the hoof' to be railed out of Marree.

POKIES
NO SMOKING
FOR SALE
LAGER
COOPERS BREWERY
PREMIUM LIGHT
DRAUGHT

XXXX
GOLD
MARREE HOTEL
MARREE HOTEL
ACCOMMODATION MEALS BARS
BOTTLE SHOP EFTPOS AVAILABLE
XXXX GOLD
DINING ROOM MEALS

Birdsville, Innamincka, Oodnadatta, repeater stations on the Telegraph Line and other far-flung destinations, received their goods from Marree via camel trains. Imported from countries such as Egypt, Turkey and Persia, these beasts of burden were utilised for all sorts of jobs, carrying wool, farming and fencing goods along with building materials for the Overland Telegraph and the railway as it pushed towards Oodnadatta and eventually to Alice Springs. The men who were skilled in handling these camel strings, although not necessarily from Afghanistan, became known as Afghans or Ghans.

By 1910 there were over 60 cameleers and 1500 camels working out of Marree. As a lasting tribute to these men and their camels the railway became known as 'The Ghan'. Camel transport had all but ended by the late 1930s.

Marree's decline commenced when motorised road trains were introduced for transportation of livestock. Droving ceased along the Birdsville Track in the 1960s, then in 1980 the last train ran along The Ghan railway line.

These days Marree is buoyed by tourists and is a popular break for adventurous travellers exploring the historic Birdsville and Oodnadatta tracks as well as Lake Eyre and the Simpson Desert.

Dating from 1883, this grand two storey hotel seems out of place in present day Marree where most of the town's buildings are simple corrugated iron structures.

Middleton Hotel

Middleton, which consists of the pub and a ramshackle public hall, was once described as 'a desperately lonely tin shelter sharing a desolate landscape with two petrified tree trunks'.

Middleton Hotel
Kennedy Developmental Road
Middleton, Queensland
(07) 4657 3980

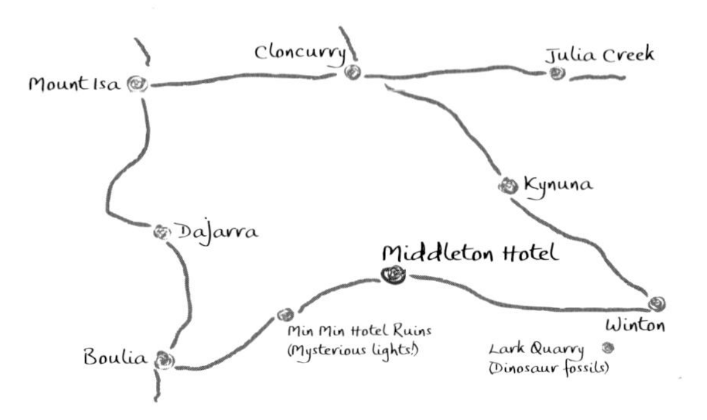

Built in 1876 by a carrier named Wiggins, the Middleton Hotel was the first of eight hotels to be built along the Boulia-Winton Road. Established during the heady times of Cobb & Co when there was a flurry of transport through these outback regions, the Middleton Hotel is the only surviving hotel along this stretch of road. The pub was used as a coaching station from 1893 until 1915.

Constructed of weatherboards with a corrugated iron roof, the Middleton Hotel is one of the few remaining intact examples of a western Queensland roadside inn, having been altered little over the years. It's a charming building sitting proudly on a vast black soil plain, the seemingly endless horizon only punctuated by scattered flat-topped rocky outcrops and the occasional stunted tree.

Frederick Henderson was granted the first licence for the hotel in 1889, and it has been licenced ever since. Over the years the hotel has been a meeting point for families from the surrounding properties, truckies, graziers, drovers, travellers, council workers and road crews.

The hotel is furnished with a traditional deep verandah and double opening doors to the interior. Inside the bar you'll find photos and stories, on the walls, of the Cobb & Co times as well as snippets of the region's early pastoral history. Out the front of the hotel is an original Cobb & Co coach. This coach was once pulled by camels on the Winton to Boulia run. There are even some old wooden hitching posts out the front which you could quite easily picture horses tied to.

HOME
MADE
COFFEE CAKE
$5-00
ROOMS
SHIRTS
Everybody needs
to believe in
something.
I believe I will
have another beer
HOTEL

MIDDLETON HOTEL
BEER · FOOD · FUEL · CAMP
"CALL IN AND RELAX"
MIDDLETON HOTEL

MENU

MIDDLETON HOTEL
BEER·FOOD·FUEL·CAMP
'CALL IN AND RELAX'
No 1
ROYAL
MAIL
COBB
VR

MIDDLETON HOTEL

BAR
MENU

MIDDLETON HOTEL
CAMP
"CALL IN AND RELAX"

Nerriga Hotel

After a dubious start as a sly grog shop and a number of interesting name changes, the Nerriga Hotel, between Nowra and Braidwood, is still dispensing refreshments to the travelling public.

Nerriga Hotel
Braidwood Road, Nerriga
New South Wales
(02) 4845 9120

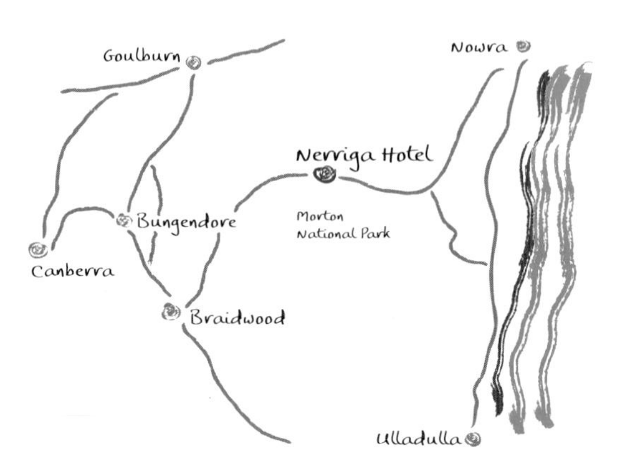

In the mid 1800s James Dunn established an illegal drinking house in the newly discovered Nerriga goldfields, but it wasn't until 1864 that the premises were officially opened as the Cricketers' Arms Hotel. Later its name was changed to the Commercial Hotel and a century after becoming licenced, in 1966, new ownership instigated yet another name change, this time to the rather intriguing Bark Tree Pub. Today, this charming single storey weatherboard and corrugated iron highland's establishment goes by the relatively straightforward name of Nerriga Hotel.

The small village of Nerriga is located high up in the coastal escarpment country along the Braidwood-Nowra Road. The road, originally known as the 'Wool Road' and built in 1841 by convict labour, saw Nerriga became an important stopover point for teamsters carting wool and other produce from Goulburn and the Monaro region to the port on Jervis Bay bound for Sydney.

Then, in 1851 after alluvial gold was discovered on the Shoalhaven River, the area grew as prospectors flocked to the new diggings. Records show that between 1878 and 1902 over 14 100 ounces of gold were taken from the area.

Today's Nerriga is a far cry from its once boisterous past. There are a few houses, a school and the hotel. Along with the born and bred locals, the many 'new settlers' who have escaped the city rat-race, add to the mix of characters you're likely to meet at the bar.

CARLTON
DRAUGHT
BREWERY FRESH
NERRIGA HOTEL
CARLTON DRAUGHT

Glenno MY PLATE '05
EXIT
PURE BLONDE
TOOHEYS NEW
TOOHEYS NEW
TOOHEYS NEW
TOOHEYS NEW
LANCER SUPER

CHILDREN WELCOME!
IF YOU ARE UNDER 18
YOU ARE BY LAW
NOT PERMITTED TO BE IN
THIS PART OF THE HOTEL
ENTER

Nindigully Pub

This rambling old bush pub on the banks of the Moonie River has long held an enviable reputation for conviviality with both locals and travellers since its early days as a coach changing station.

Nindigully Pub
Sternes Street, Nindigully
Queensland
(07) 4625 9637

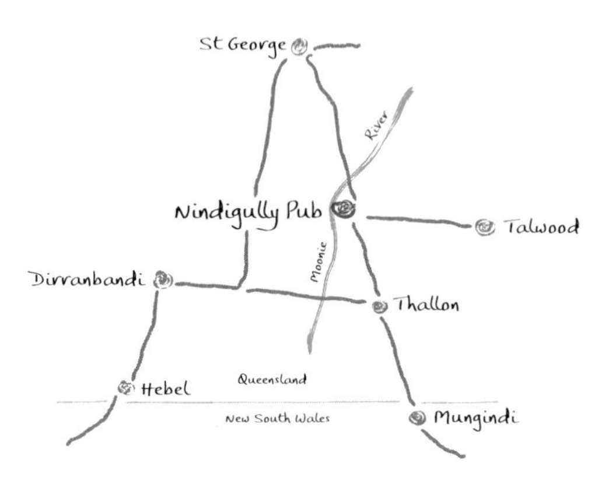

Nindigully Pub is an imposing wooden building with a wide wrap-around verandah and shady beer garden. Set in a picturesque location, it looks out over the tree-lined Moonie River.

Established in 1864, it is said that the building was originally shearer's quarters on Nindigully Station prior to becoming a coach changing station and then a pub. It is believed the hotel, which is still in its original location, holds the longest continual licence in Queensland.

Inside, the pub is bursting with character. There's a main bar with the now almost obligatory hat collection on the wall, saddles, posters, the skin of a 'Nindigully Geko', mounted animal heads and various curios from around the district. There's also an interesting assortment of framed newspaper and magazine tear sheets adorning one of the walls. The bar counter tops are massive timber slabs while the original rough-sawn timber floorboards on the verandah add to the pub's rustic appeal. A delightful timber lined dining room is just off the bar, and it too has many black and white photographs on the walls from the town's heyday.

In 1862 a once-weekly mail run commenced from Surat, running south to Mungindi on the New South Wales/Queensland border. It followed the Balonne River through St George to Nindigully. At Nindigully the route crossed the Moonie River prior to continuing on to Mungindi. This route was also used by cattlemen droving stock north from New South Wales into Queensland's newly settled western downs.

NO QUICK SERVICE AT THE GULLY
McWILLIAM'S
Cream
PORT
Rich Smooth Fruity
XXXX
SOUVENIRS
XXXX GOLD
HAPPY HOUR
ALLIS-CHALMERS
BEER IS OUR FRIEND
GOOD AS GOLD

Rich Smooth Fruity...
PORT
THAT REMINDS ME
It's All Right!
FOUREX
FOUREX THE POPULAR BEER
Queensland!
XXXX
GOLD
LAGER
SOLVOL
cleans
hands
quickly
BALONNE BEACON
The Pub with no beer
Simply the best
Courier Mail
Chronicle

With the increase of stock movements and the population growth in the early 1860s, as people pushed up from the south, there came a need for commercial premises to supply the necessary services of food and accommodation.

The first of the region's hotels appeared in Mungindi and St George, with Nindigully being the next locale to be issued a licence for a hotel. In September 1864 Thomas Bradford became publican of the aptly named Nindigully Hotel.

As the use of the route from Mungindi to St George continued to flourish, a timber bridge was constructed in 1885 to cross the Moonie River. Although no longer in use, the old bridge still spans the river opposite the hotel.

The licence changed to James Roger in June 1876 and the name changed to the Travellers Rest Hotel. After this time there were three more name changes, including The Sportsmans Arms, before it reverted to its original name of Nindigully Hotel. There have been a total of 23 licensees of the hotel since Thomas Bradford.

These days the main road bypasses Nindigully, which is made up of the pub, a couple of houses, the old General Store and a town hall. The town's permanent population is six!

New Year's Eve is one of the biggest nights of the year in Nindigully with people coming from far and wide to join in the celebrations.

PUB
EST.1884

Noccundra Hotel

Noccundra Hotel was established to serve thirsty station workers from surrounding pastoral stations, as well as teamsters carting supplies and drovers plying the southern stock routes.

Noccundra Hotel
Wilson Street, Noccundra
Queensland
(07) 4655 4317

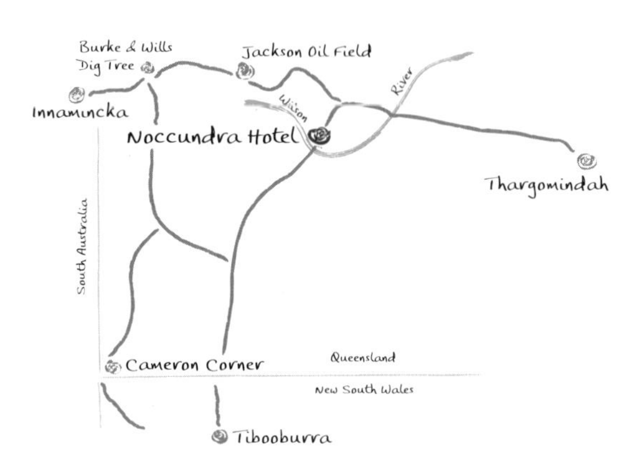

It is believed that the current Noccundra Hotel replaced an earlier rough shanty pub which traded on the site from about the late 1860s, around the time of the establishment of Nockatunga Station.

Located opposite a permanent waterhole on the Wilson River, Noccundra was at the intersection of stock routes south to Tibooburra in New South Wales and west into South Australia on the Cooper Creek. It soon became a well received resting place for drovers to spell stock.

There are no records as to who built the present building, but James Gardiner held the first licence from 1883. The handsome, single storey sandstone building, which comprises of a bar room with an adjacent dining room, complete with open fire, is heritage listed.

A town reserve was created in 1885 and by the end of 1889 consisted of a store and police station, along with the hotel.

Henry Hughes, the then owner of Nockatunga Station, purchased both the store and hotel in 1915. The store traded up until 1933, and then in 1959 the police station closed. The township of Noccundra never really eventuated, although the hotel has continued to trade since being licenced, serving stockmen, workers from the surrounding gas and oil fields as well as travellers.

The hotel stayed in the ownership of the Hughes family until 1991, when Nockatunga Station, along with the hotel – which is on land owned by Nockatunga – was purchased by the Packer family's Australian Consolidated Pastoral Co.

NOCCUNDRA HOTEL

Looking for Leichhardt

In 1848 Prussian-born explorer Ludwig Leichhardt and his party vanished without trace somewhere in northern Australia in an attempt to traverse Australia from east to west. Leichhardt was an experienced bushman and navigator. The disappearance of the fully provisioned party still remains a mystery. They were last seen at Cogoon Station near Roma.

In 1874 Andrew Hume, following a stint in Parramatta Goal for robbery, set off in search of Leichhardt. Hume claimed that in 1862 he had meet one of the exploring party, a man by the name of Classen, living with Aboriginals in the Victoria River area of northern Australia. Hume said he was unable to persuade the white man, who was in possession of papers proving his identity, to come with them.

Timothy O'Hea and Lewis Thompson joined the party after other men had pulled out, and along with Hume headed for Cooper Creek en route to Victoria River. At Nockatunga Station on the Wilson River, near Noccundra, Hume and his group took a wrong turn, taking them into the rugged foothills of the Grey Range, away from water. While Thompson found his way back to a creek, both Hume and O'Hea perished from thirst.

A monument to Hume and his party is located at the hotel.

Along with Thompson and O'Hea, Hume became embattled in a struggle for survival to the west of remote Nockatunga Station.

XXXX

Ora Banda Inn

Overland Corner Hotel

Ora Banda Inn

The name Ora Banda was bestowed by the Weston brothers, who wanted a distinctive title for their newly established mine. As a name, Ora Banda has a rich ring to it.

Ora Banda Inn
Gimlet Street, Ora Banda
Western Australia
(08) 9024 2444

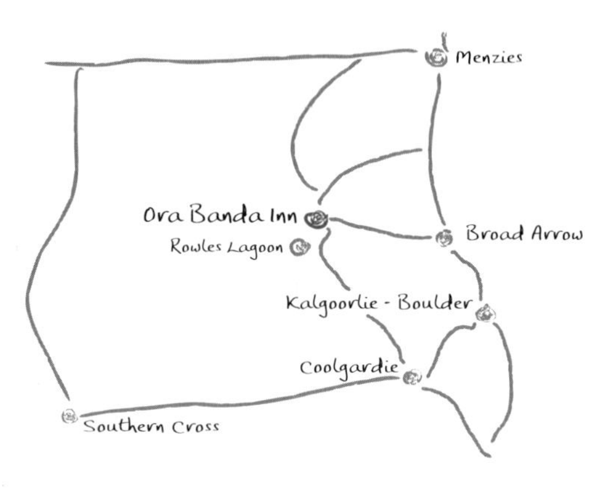

In 1906 a township site was established near newly discovered ore bodies north-west of Kalgoorlie. The town took its name from a nearby mine which was worked by the Weston brothers. Ora Banda, roughly translated in Spanish means band, or sash of gold.

As more gold strikes were made, Ora Banda's population steadily increased and by 1910 there were 2000 people living in the town. Unlike many other fields, Ora Banda's continuing prosperity seemed assured and in 1911 Alfred Garnett built the Ora Banda Hotel. Constructed of brick and stone, Garnett must have been confident that Ora Banda would develop into a major centre, unlike many other goldfield towns which disappeared almost as quickly as they were established.

The hotel traded for the next 40 years, riding the wave as the mining boom fluctuated. The government built battery helped to stave off the inevitable, but by the late 1950s Ora Banda was little more than a ghost town. The hotel closed.

In 1981, the derelict hotel, now only a shell, was restored by Albert Klaassen and reopened to cater for the new mining operations in the area.

In 1995 Don Hancock and his family took over the hotel and in October 2000 the building was bombed. The hotel once again closed.

Two years later the hotel again reopened and then closed after 11 months.

The Ora Banda Inn lay idle for another 18 months before reopening in 2006. It is still trading and is a popular day trip from Kalgoorlie.

menu
TOOHEYS
EXTRA DRY
SWAN
DRAUGHT
XXXX
GOLD
SWAN

ORABANDA
OPEN

The Ora Banda Bombings

In October 2000, a series of events unfolded in and around the Ora Banda Inn, including a murder and a number of fire bombings.

When former CIB head Don Hancock took over the Ora Banda Inn in 1995 it was a well frequented watering hole and continued so for the next five years, attracting locals as well as travellers. Hancock also had mining interests in the area, including the old state-owned battery. But that was all about to change.

On the afternoon of October 1st, 2000 a small group of Gypsy Joker motorcyclists rode into town, and after setting up camp at the nearby racetrack, headed to the hotel. Apparently, after a time, there was an altercation between Hancock and one of the group, Billy Grierson, after which Hancock insisted that Grierson and his mates leave the pub. Shortly after, back at the Gypsy Jokers camp, Grierson was shot in the back. He died shortly afterwards. Nobody saw the gunman.

In the ensuing weeks, the hotel was fire bombed on two occasions, as was Hancock's house and the state battery. The Hancocks quit Ora Banda and returned to Perth.

Then in September 2001, Hancock and a mate, Lou Lewis were killed when their car exploded from a car bomb as Hancock pulled into the driveway of his Perth home.

A section of pressed metal wall from the bombing has been kept and can still be seen at the Ora Banda Inn.

Nuggets For Sale

Overland Corner Hotel

This classic colonial inn, reputedly the oldest surviving hotel to be built along the Murray River, has had a colourful past, hosting patrons ranging from bushrangers to ghosts.

Overland Corner Hotel
Old Coach Road
Overland Corner
South Australia
(08) 8588 7021

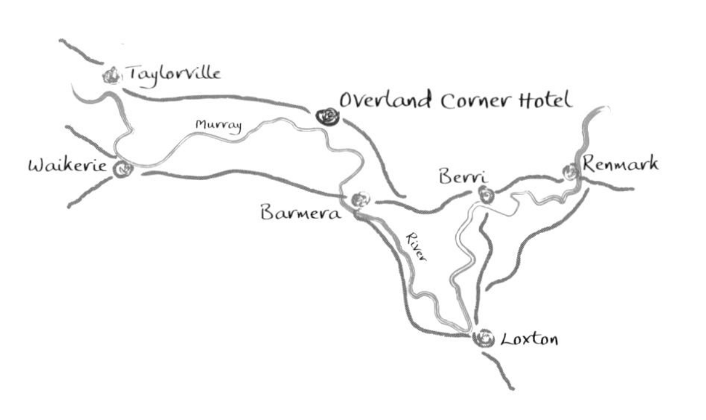

The Overland Corner Hotel was built by the Brand brothers in 1859 for pastoralist, John Chambers. Using local materials, it was constructed of limestone blocks hewn from a nearby quarry, local red gum and native Murray pine timbers and a thatched roof of river reeds. One of the brothers, William, was the hotel's first licensee.

The hotel originally sat on land which was part of Chambers' Cobdogla Station, a sprawling cattle property on the Murray River. The 'overland corner' refers to the river bend where large mobs of cattle were swum across the river after drovers had moved them 'overland' from New South Wales, destined for the Adelaide markets. The extensive river flat below the hotel was used as a holding paddock for stock, while no doubt, many a drover enjoyed the pub's hospitality. Today it's a popular camping area.

The pub operated for almost 40 years before being delicenced in 1897. It operated as a store and post office until 1965 when the property was bought by the National Trust and restored to its former glory. It was relicenced as a hotel in 1987.

Like most good pubs, The Overland Corner Hotel is not without a swag of yarns. Irishman Andrew Scott, otherwise known as bushranger Captain Moonlight, is alleged to have had a drink or two at the hotel with a few accomplices. Moonlight is said to have rode his horse into the front bar. Ghosts of past patrons are also said to still enjoy the pub's hospitality, revelling into the early hours, long after the lights are out!

HISTORIC OVERLAND CORNER HOTEL
OVERLAND CORNER HOTEL
1860
Entrance
MIRANDA WINES
BOOKINGS ESSENTIAL
LUNCH
Tues-Sun 12-2pm
DINNER
6-8pm

LIQUOR LICENSING ACT 1997
LIQUOR MUST NOT BE SUPPLIED TO PERSONS UNDER 18.
STOP
PERSONS UNDER 18 NOT TO ENTER. THIS AREA IS OUT OF BOUNDS TO A PERSON UNDER 18 BETWEEN MIDNIGHT ON ONE DAY AND 5:00AM OF THE NEXT. PERSONS SUSPECTED OF BEING UNDER 18 MAY BE REQUIRED TO PROVIDE EVIDENCE OF THEIR AGE.
OLD COACH RD
Restrooms
Hot Drinks
Tea or Coffee $2.00
Hot Chocolate $2.50
Espresso $2.50
Mocha Latte $2.50
Plunger Coffee
Muffins
Homemade Scones

B

Royal Hotel - Bedourie

Royal Hotel - Eromanga

Royal Mail Hotel

Royal Hotel - Bedourie

Bedourie is situated in the south-west corner of Queensland on a vast gibber strewn plain and surrounded by sandhills. The sole remaining pub, the Royal, has served the town continuously since 1886.

Royal Hotel
Herbert Street, Bedourie
Queensland
(07) 4746 1201

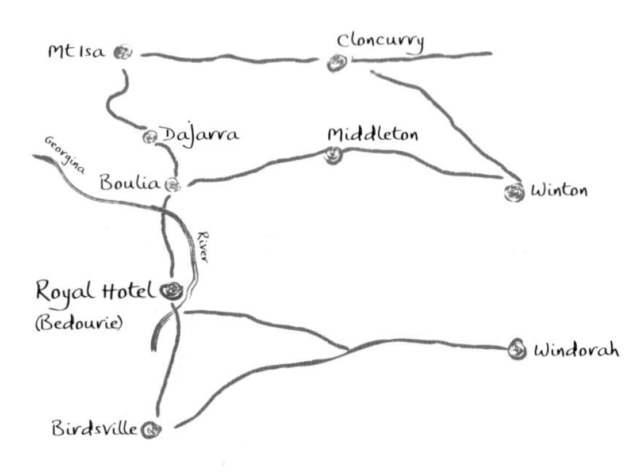

Bedourie grew from a shanty settlement located on the main north-south stock route which linked stations in the north of Queensland and the Northern Territory to Marree in South Australia.

Of the town's two hotels, The Royal was built sometime during 1886 to serve the growing community. It was constructed of kiln-fired mud bricks – as opposed to the more common method of sun drying – a task which took almost two years to complete. The hotel's first licensee was James Craigie, who ran the pub with his wife.

As the 1800s drew to a close Bedourie had cemented its position as an important supply centre for grazing properties throughout the Channel Country. It had also become a well established stopover for drovers using the Georgina Stock Route. Bedourie is now the administrative centre for the Diamantina Shire.

The Royal Hotel was gutted by fire in the early 1900s, sustaining substantial damage. It was subsequently rebuilt using local stone but retained some of the original brickwork. The thatched roof was replaced with corrugated iron. In later years a boundary workers' hut from Ethabuka Spring was added to the hotel and now serves as the dining room.

Today, the exterior of the hotel retains a classic bush pub character with its pitched corrugated iron roof, thick masonry walls and large verandah. Inside there is a main bar at one end with an open fireplace built into the opposing wall. There is a dining room in the back section of the hotel.

VICTORIA VB BITTER
WETSUIT
VB VICTORIA BITTER
For a hard earned thirst

VICTORIA
VB
BITTER
For a hard
earned thirst
CARLTON
MID
$88.88

GOLD

CARLTON MID
Bottle Shop:-
6 Pack (Light/Heavy) $15
12 Light $25
12 Heavy $27
Carlton Light
Baileys
Jack Daniels
Jim Beam
Johnnie Walker
Kahlua
Midori
Vodka
Tobacco:-
VICTORIA BITTER
VB
WETSUIT
ATTENTION
For a hard earned thirst
Wrangler
XXXX GOLD
CARLTON MID

The Bedourie Oven

Bedourie lends its name to a simple, but ingenious piece of outback cookware, the Bedourie Camp Oven.

During the late 1800s through to the early 1900s, drover's cooks mostly used cast iron camp ovens to cook any matter of fare from the humble damper – a staple in bush camps – to stews and desserts. Cast iron was heavy, awkward to stow and carry on pack horses as well as brittle; it often cracked when dropped.

It is thought that a bagman, 'on the wallaby' during the Great Depression of the 1930s had come to the Bedourie area looking for work. A tin-smith by trade, the bagman set about fashioning flat sided billy cans along with a number of steel camp ovens. These were stocked by Alan Gaffney's pub store in Bedourie and soon became popular with droving outfits passing through the area. The practical utensil soon gained the name of the 'Bedourie Oven'.

In 1945 RM Williams had this style of camp oven made of pressed steel and in the 1960s had the item listed in his mail-order catalogue as a Bedourie Camp Oven.

These lightweight, unbreakable spun steel camp ovens – the fitting lid can be used as a frypan – are still in use by bush cooks today.

The Post Office still operates from the Royal Hotel, like it has done for many years.

Royal Hotel - Eromanga

Famous for being Australia's furthest town from the ocean, Eromanga once boasted three hotels and was on a well-travelled Cobb & Co route until the advent of motorised transport.

Royal Hotel
Deacon Street, Eromanga
Queensland
(07) 4656 4837

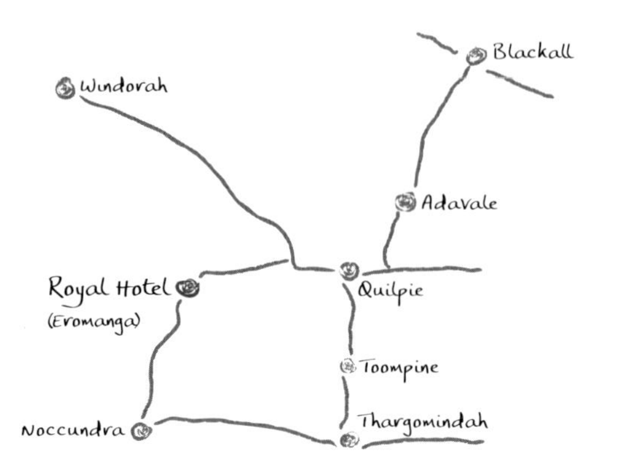

In the early 1870s a settlement by the name of 'Opal Opolis' formed in the locality of a shanty pub popularly called the 'Round House'. Established to service the opal miners at the Little Wonder mines on Mt Margaret Station, in March 1879 the settlement was gazetted as the town of Eromanga, reputedly an Aboriginal word meaning 'Windy Plain'. Even today, the dust swirls around the town as the winds whip in across the sweeping plains from all points of the compass.

At its peak Eromanga supported three hotels, The Royal, The Australian and The Grand. Only the Royal survived and remains open today. First licenced to William McGill in 1886 and constructed of handmade mud bricks, The Royal operated as a Cobb & Co changing station – it was the second last stop on the Kyabra run – as well as being a favoured watering hole for the large shearing teams which regularly passed through the area. Opal buyers coming from the south to purchase the precious stone also used the hotel.

Of the other hotels, The Australian closed its doors in the early 1900s and The Grand was a short lived venture, only being licenced for a few years. In addition to the hotels there were two stores, a school, a police station, a blacksmith shop next to The Royal Hotel and a Chinese market garden beside Euronghoola Creek.

The Royal Hotel is a neat, well kept outback pub. A shady verandah shelters the front while behind the massively thick walls is a cosy front bar with a lounge bar located off to the side.

Est. 1885
ROYAL HOTEL
'EROMANGA'
The furthest town from the sea.
ROYAL HOTEL
PUBLIC BAR
XXX
SUPER

Royal Mail Hotel

First licenced in 1874, Hungerford's delightfully charming Royal Mail Hotel has provided refreshments and accommodation to the travelling public for over 135 years.

Royal Mail Hotel
Archernar Street, Hungerford
Queensland
(07) 4655 4093

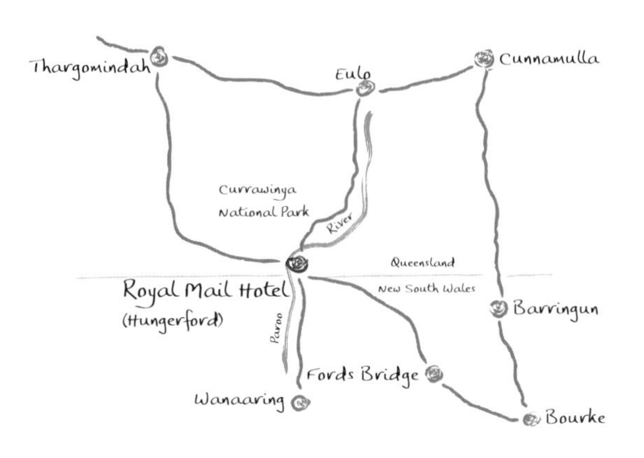

The border township of Hungerford came into being in the early 1870s and was gazetted in 1875. It takes its name from Thomas Hungerford, an Irishman who held substantial grazing properties in the area. Hungerford administered these holdings from his base in the Hunter Valley of New South Wales and often camped beside the Paroo River on his visits to his Queensland properties at a site which became known as 'Hungerford's Camp'.

The Royal Mail Hotel was thought to have been established around the time of the original township and was first licenced in 1874. Another hotel, The Commercial, no longer exists.

Built from timber and corrugated iron, the Royal Mail is practically in original condition – this is one of the few bush pubs with its authentic originality still in tact. There are shady verandahs around two sides, and at the front corner is the doorway into the bar. Wooden floorboards, wood lined walls and a high ceiling, again lined with wood, all add to the atmosphere inside the hotel. Adjoining the front bar is a small dining room with a delightful open fireplace, throughout the pub there are interesting memorabilia on the walls along with snippets about the hotel's history.

The Royal Mail was a changing station for Cobb & Co on the Bourke to Thargomindah/ Cunnamulla route. Passengers would have a meal and overnight at the hotel.

Today, the mail contract is still held by the hotel, with the publican delivering mail to the town and surrounding properties.

TO LET.
FEMALES ONLY!
ICECREAM
HEARTS
DRUM STICK
MONACO
Quitline
13 QUIT
FERTILIZE THE BUSH
DOZE IN A GREENIE
NO SMOKING

POST
POST
BUS STOP

ROYAL MAIL
HOTEL
MEAT
SMALLGOODS

ROYAL MAIL HOTEL
The First Fleet
SIMPLE IN USE
EFFECTIVE IN SERVICE
YOU ARE UNDER 18
YOU ARE NOT
PERMITTED
VISA

Henry Lawson's Hungerford

In the sweltering, drought-stricken summer of 1892-93 bush poet Henry Lawson tramped the well-worn track from Bourke to Hungerford in search of stories. He'd been given a train ticket to Bourke and a £5 note by FJ Archibald, editor of the *Bulletin* magazine, to head bush in search of work and to send back copy for the magazine.

Lawson later wrote in *Hungerford,* one of a collection of stories published in *While the Billy Boils,* 'Hungerford consists of two houses and a humpy in New South Wales and five houses in Queensland. Characteristically enough, both the pubs are in Queensland. We got a glass of sour yeast at one and paid sixpence for it – we had asked for English ale. The Post Office is in New South Wales, and the police-barracks in Bananaland. The police cannot do anything if there is a row going on across the street in New South Wales, except send to Brisbane and have an extradition warrant applied for; and they don't do much if there is a row in Queensland. Most of the rows are across the border in Queensland, where the pubs are.'

Lawson went on to write 'Next morning we rolled up our swags and left Hungerford to the North-West'.

Lawson vowed 'never to face the bush again' and returned to Sydney.

The pub's underground cellar still exists with shelves dug from the earth on which the wooden kegs of beer would have been stored.

SILVERTON HOTEL
SOFALA ROYAL HOTEL
SOUTH WESTERN HOTEL

Silverton Hotel

Australia's most photographed pub, the Silverton Hotel has appeared in countless TV commercials as well as box office block-busters like Mad Max II, but despite the fame, it's still a top outback boozer.

Silverton Hotel
Layard Street, Silverton
New South Wales
(08) 8088 5313

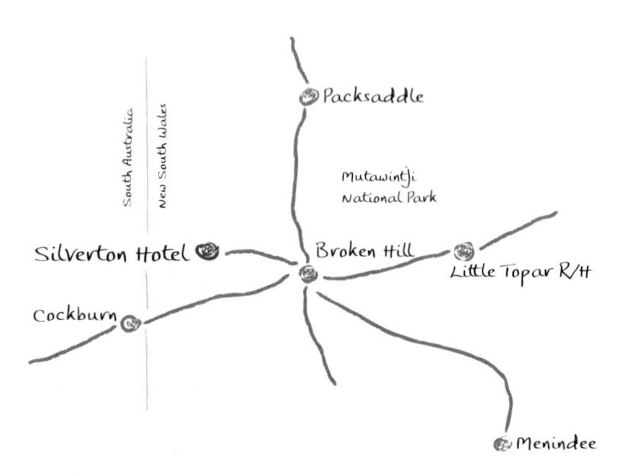

Once a mining town, Silverton – which is a little over 20 kilometres north-west of Broken Hill – is pretty much famous for its pub. Along with a few houses, a couple of churches and an old gaol, there is a small colony of painters and other artisans, many with galleries displaying their wares.

The current Silverton Hotel was built in 1885 and is the last remaining of ten licenced premises which serviced, what was then, Australia's richest silver field. At its peak the town had three breweries, one of which was operated by Emil Resch who afterwards founded Resch's Brewery in Sydney.

Over the years there have been three hotels in town going by the name of Silverton Hotel. The first was the De Baun Silverton Hotel – a single storey building built in April 1883. The next was a two storey building erected in 1884, while the current building dates from 1885. Interestingly, all three buildings were built alongside each other.

They must have been a thirsty lot at Silverton back in the 1880s. Local records suggest that when John De Baun swung open the pub's doors for the first time, the drinkers poured nineteen tons of beer down their parched throats in the hotel's first four weeks of operation!

The pub is still essentially a drinking spot for locals and tourists. Constructed from stone and brick with an iron roof, it's a solid looking structure. Inside there is a large bar room with an open fire down one end and scattered around the walls is a collection of memorabilia.

SILVERTON HOTEL

Hollywood of the Outback

Estimated to having been viewed by 500 million people throughout the world, The Silverton Hotel has featured in a string of television series and successful films including: *Wake in Fright, The Golden Soak, A Town Like Alice, Mad Max II* starring Mel Gibson, *Hostage, Razorback, Blue Lightning, Ricky and Pete, Dirty Deeds* and Jimeoin's *The Craic.*

The variety of scenery close to town, along with the similarity of the region to other locations in more remote parts of Australia are major factors in Silverton's popularity with film-makers. Add to this the availability of accommodation for large film crews and access to building materials for set construction in nearby Broken Hill, and of course, the bright, sunny weather conditions throughout the year, and you have an ideal cinematographic location.

Over the years the pub has been used by film-makers as a hotel, American diner and coffee shops. The pub has 'appeared' as the Nullagine Hotel in *The Golden Soak,* Hotel Australia in *A Town Like Alice,* Mulga Mulga Hotel in numerous XXXX beer commercials, the Dingo Hotel in *As Time Goes By,* Chuck's Diner in an Eveready Battery commercial, the Mundi Mundi Hotel for a Carling beer commercial and Federal Hotel in the movie *Dirty Deeds.*

...where men outnumbered women by 50 to 1 – the miners sought solace at the bars and hotels which appeared like magic in dry, dusty Silverton.

OLD
XXXX
GOLD
HAHN

Sofala Royal Hotel

Sofala is Australia's oldest remaining gold town, dating from 1851. The village's narrow streets house an array of unique period buildings, including the charming Sofala Royal Hotel.

Sofala Royal Hotel
Denison Street, Sofala
New South Wales
(02) 6337 7008

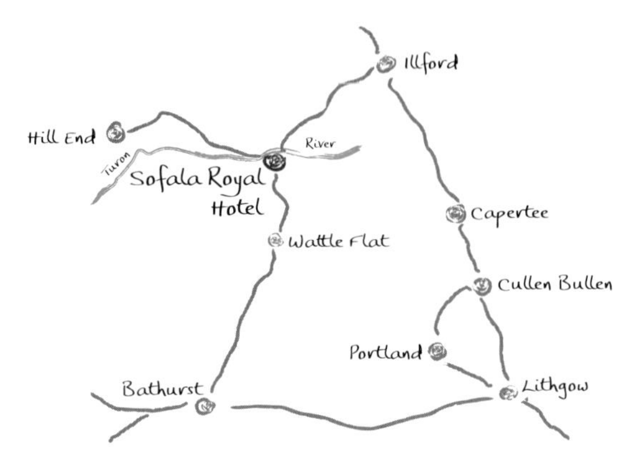

Following the discovery of gold on the Turon River in 1851, a frenetic rush to the area soon saw the establishment of the settlement of Sofala. Set amongst the expanding alluvial workings, this early township, which consisted mostly of canvas tents and bark huts, was spread out along the river west for five kilometres to Wallaby Rocks and a similar distance to the east to Upper Turon. Before long churches, schools, a court of petty sessions, a hospital and many other businesses sprang into existence, servicing this fast growing area.

At the height of gold fever in the mid 1860s there were 50 licenced hotels – although most would have been little more than two roomed shacks – on the fields, along with an estimated 500 illegal sly grog shanties serving the population which was thought to number over 30 000 European diggers and 10 000 Chinese prospectors, all searching for their fortune. The village benefited from its position on the main road between Bathurst and the Hunter region, and the fact that the gold lasted much longer than in many other regions.

Of all the town's pubs, only the Sofala Royal Hotel remains licenced. The two storey weatherboard pub with its impressive wrought-iron balcony, opened at the height of the rush and has traded continuously since becoming first licenced in 1862, except for a brief period in 1940. A number of other hotels are now private dwellings.

The hotel's first proprietor was European immigrant Moritz Mendel and his wife Anne. Anne died during childbirth in 1877 and Moritz

SOFALA ROYAL HOTEL
BAR

is said to have committed suicide in the hotel – five years after the death of his wife and child – in room 6, which is now used as a guestroom. Moritz must have found solace by his own hand as there are no reports that he haunts the hotel after all these years.

Like many hotels of this era, it has a connection to the famous Cobb & Co. The far end of the bar, in use today, was once part of a coach booking office. There were regular daily coach services to and from Bathurst as well as a service north to Mudgee and beyond.

As the gold began to peter out the miners and their families moved to other fields – a new strike at Wattle Flat attracted a lot of Sofala's population while others flocked to new finds at Palmers Oaky and Spring Creek. By the early 1870s Sofala's population had declined markedly, although the town managed to survive despite the exodus. Mining, mostly by large, well funded ventures – including dredges on the Turon River – continued in the area until just before World War I, with sporadic small-scale bursts up until the 1950s.

These days Sofala offers a window into the past. The hotel remains much the same as it would have been during the town's heyday, and is one of the few licenced goldfields pubs from this early time still serving thirsty visitors.

In 1986 floodwaters from the swollen Turon River inundated the hotel, but luckily they receded quickly, saving the hotel's bottom storey from ruin.

Bushells
Coffee
Blue Label
Bushells
Mariners
BAR
Smoking kills
Call the Quitline
131 848
TOOHEYS
Here's To'ee
USHERS
SPECIAL RESERVE
TOOHEYS
OATMEAL
STOUT

South Western Hotel

Once a welcome respite for local graziers, opal miners and travelling shearing teams – many of them on pushbikes – along the Quilpie to Thargomindah road, the 'Toompine Pub' is a still popular venue today.

South Western Hotel
Stanley Street, Toompine
Queensland
(07) 4656 4863

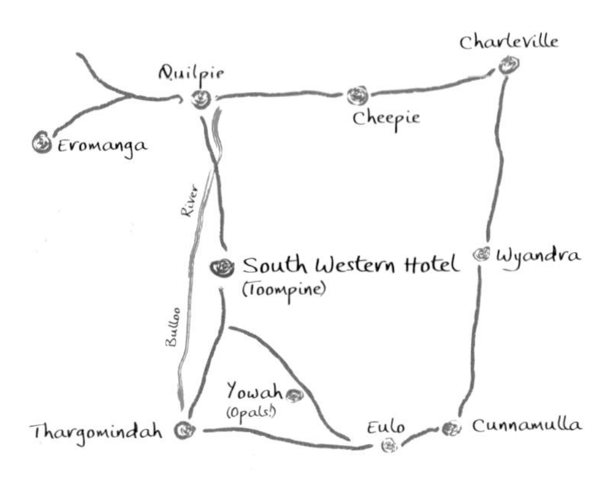

Established in the 1860s, this little western Queensland pub on the Cobb & Co run from Thargomindah to Cheepie, is where passengers overnighted and horses were changed. As time went by a small community formed, with the pub becoming a popular drinking spot for station hands, opal miners and shearing teams. It is now a well regarded stopover with travellers. The name Toompine is thought to have come from the Aboriginal 'thuenpin', meaning leech.

All that now remains, along with a hall, is the South Western Hotel, generally known as 'The Toompine Pub'. This is the second pub to stand on this site; the first hotel was destroyed by fire. The present hotel was built in 1893 by Mr Power and constructed of cypress pine and ripple iron.

The first known publican at Toompine was John Webber of Kyabra Station. Webber was also a partner in the Peppin Opal Mine. There are suggestions that Webber built the first hotel, although by 1866 a Mrs Scanlan is recorded as being the owner.

The early 1900s opal boom saw hundreds of miners flocking to the Duck Creek and Copperella fields. The only pub in a hundred miles to spend their new won fortunes was at Toompine, and no doubt they did a roaring trade. It was at Duck Creek that Queensland's largest opal the 'Huns Head' was found in 1972, weighing in at 15.75kg.

The South Western has received some renovations and extensions over the last few years, but still retains much of its former character.

TOOMPINE HOTEL MENU
CHICKEN SNITZEL
CHICKEN PARM
FISH
RUMP STEAK
MIXED GRILL
SEAFOOD BASKET
SAUSAGES ONION GRAVY
BOWL OF CHIPS
Cup of Gravy
LASAGNE
VEAL SNITZEL
TAKE AWAY MENU
FISH
CHICKO ROLL
SPRING ROLL
DIM SIMS
POTATO SCOLLOP
CHIPS
WING DINGS
HAMBURGER
STEAK SANDWICH
CHICKEN SNITZEL
TOASTED S/WCH
PIE
Pie & Chips $6
TONIGHT
MEATLOAF & VEGI $10
Johnnie Walker
BITCH
HELL
Quitline
13 QUIT
AKUBRA

VB VICTORIA BITTER
Every Family Needs A
FARMER
DAXY'S BAR

PURE BLONDE
NAKED
Bundaberg
dark storm
XXXX
GOLD

TOOMPINE
NO
DRINKING
TILL
AFTER
FIVE

TOOMPINE
SOUTH WESTERN HOTEL
LICENSEE: G. J. DAX

TOOMPINE
SOUTH WESTERN HOTEL
LICENSEE: G. J. DAX
TOOMPINE
ANGLE PARKING
ANY ANGLE
ICE

BIRDSVILLE
CEMERY 1K
TOOMPINE
SOUTH WESTERN HOTEL
LICENSEE: G. J. DAX

GRAHAM ROSE GUNDAGAI PAM BURK GUNDAGAI

WENDY & BARRIE ISAAC

TROY PAYNE

Tony Lawlence

BATEMAN'S DAY

27/5/02

Roy MCKELL

NICOLE CARTERS & TROY MACKAY "02"

MARLENE SMITH MURWILLUMBAH 02 ALAN

TRISH Bedourie

TROY

ASH. 2002

11·1·02G

JOHN & MAUREEN DODD

Stevens 2002

DE GROOT 2001

PAUL GROSE

THALIA 2001

NSW PART OFF

KAR RALLY

08-08-04

Kelly and Mark

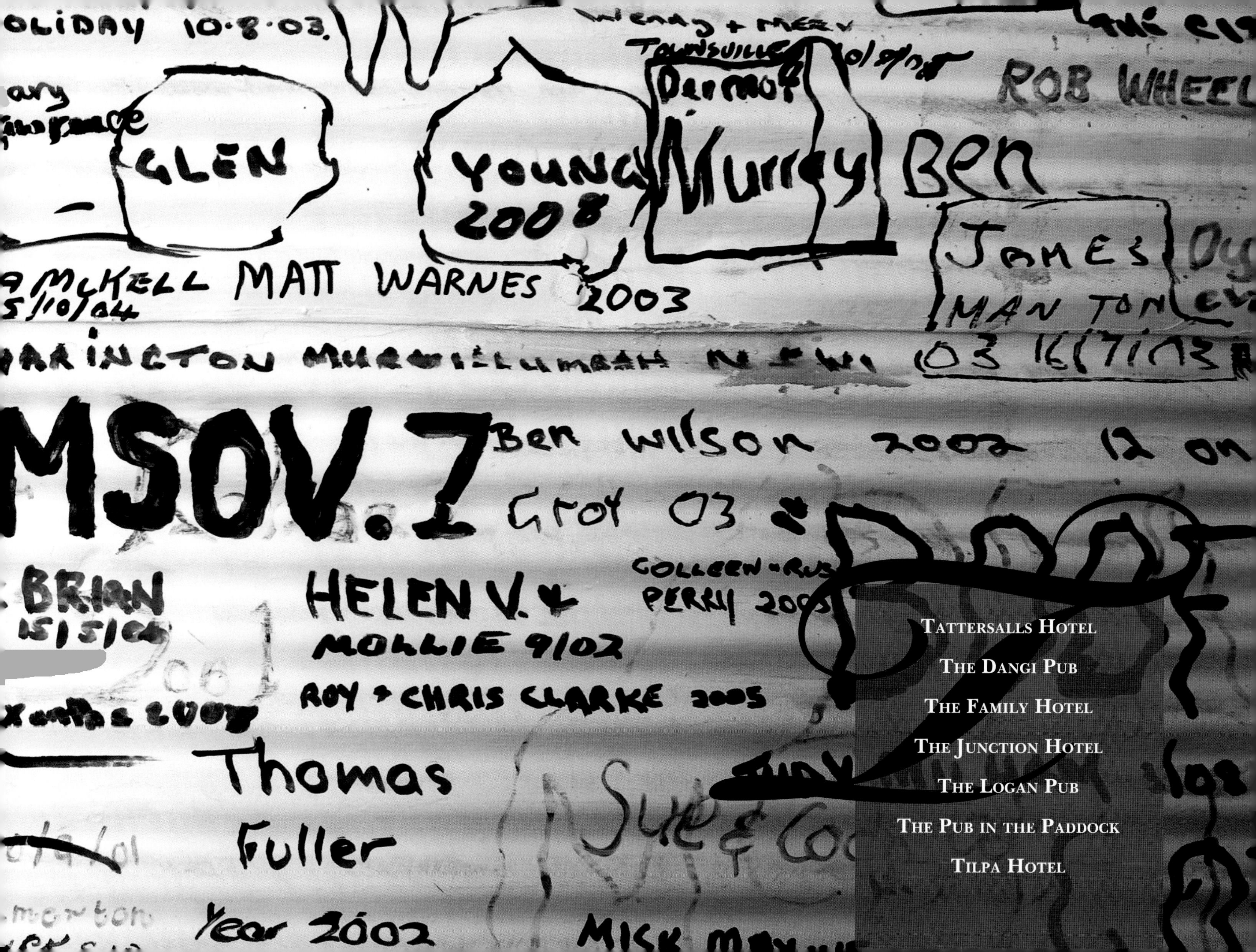

Tattersalls Hotel

The Dangi Pub

The Family Hotel

The Junction Hotel

The Logan Pub

The Pub in the Paddock

Tilpa Hotel

Tattersalls Hotel

This delightful watering hole at the border crossing at Barringun has had only three owners in its 100 year history and has been a landmark for travellers since its days as a Cobb & Co station.

Tattersalls Hotel
Mitchell Hwy, Barringun
New South Wales
(02) 6874 7588

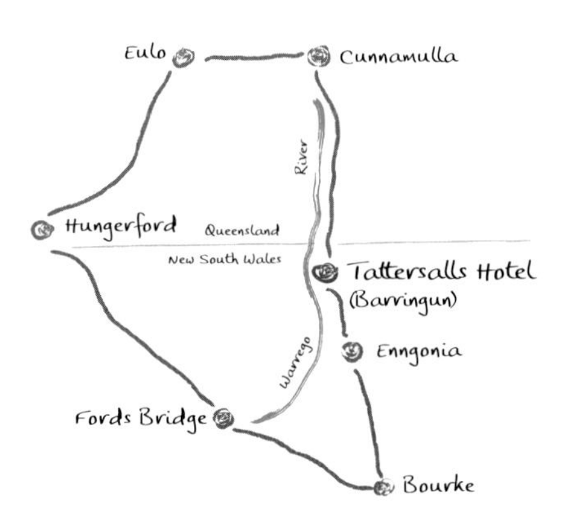

Drive along the Mitchell Highway, and just before hitting the Queensland border there's a sign which catches your eye, simply stating 'The Last Pub in NSW'. It's the Tattersalls Hotel.

The 'Tatts' was one of four pubs in the early days of Barringun, catering for all manner of bush workers. It was also a change station for Cobb & Co on the run between Bourke – the terminus for the railway – and Port Douglas.

In the late 1890s – the town's heyday – Barringun had a population of about 130 people and boasted a bank, two butcher shops, courthouse and gaol, bonded warehouse as well as a number of dwellings. At the border crossing there was a customs house. Now the population swings between three and four people.

Perched on the western side of the highway, the Tattersalls Hotel is a rather inviting looking building, but you could easily be remiss in thinking the plain facade is not the pub. The public area of the hotel consists of one bar room, and it's changed little from when first built. A grandfather clock in the corner of the bar has been there since 1938!

Publican Mary Crawley and her husband moved to the hotel in 1977, and Mary has been behind the bar ever since. Then the pub was a popular stop for truckies, calling in for a drink on their highway runs. But drink driving regulations changed all this, although Mary still gets a few interstater's from the old days dropping in to say hello.

Mary is a master in the art of conversation – there's no television in the bar at this pub.

NSW - QLD
POLICE ANNUAL
CRICKET DAY
BARRINGUN
THIS IS DEDICATED
TO THOSE SPLENDID
FELLOWS WHO MAKE
DRINKING A
PLEASURE WHO
REACH
CONTENTMENT
PRIOR TO
CAPACITY AND
WHATEVER THE
DRINK, CAN HOLD IT
AND REMAIN
GENTLEMEN
VICTORIA
BITTER
VICTORIA
VB
BITTER

The Dangi Pub

This friendly bush pub, south-west of Mt Isa, was once a haunt for Georgina Stock Route drovers, and for those willing to venture off the beaten track it offers a taste of the 'real' Queensland outback.

The Dangi Pub
Main Street, Urandangi
Queensland
(07) 4748 4988

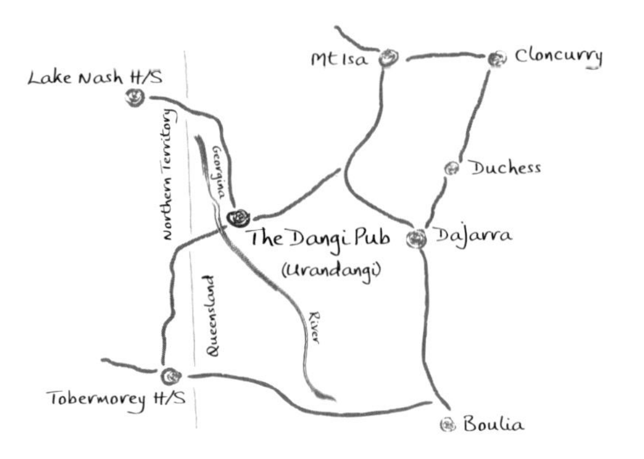

At one time the small settlement of Urandangi was an important rest stop along the Georgina Stock Route, and the hotel was one of the most popular with droving plants who brought thousands of head of cattle down from the Barkly Tableland. The droving days are long gone and the town now exists in quieter times.

Urandangi was founded by James Hutton and Charles Webster, who set up as storekeepers in this remote outpost in 1885 to service the trade along the stock route. Today the store is closed, but the Urandangi Hotel, or 'The Dangi Pub' as it is known to most, survives, and along with a few houses, makes up the town.

Located on the edge of a sweeping plain and not far from the Georgina River channels, the settlement has an almost quintessential remoteness which typifies far western Queensland.

The original pub burned to the ground in 1932, but was soon replaced when the old hospital building from Kuridala was relocated some 130 kilometres – as the crow flys – to Urandangi after the former tin mining town, to the south of Cloncurry, was abandoned.

The Dangi Pub is a great example of north western Queensland vernacular building style. Constructed of timber with a corrugated iron roof, it has a wide, shady verandah all around. Inside, the original floorboards add a depth of character to the hotel which consists of a timber lined bar room and a dining room. There is a tree shaded beer garden out the back.

EXIT
Bread
Pies
ICE

MIDSTRENGTH
VICTORIA BITTER

MARCH 97
URANDANGI
No more. It's the Law.

RUM
XXXX
GOLD

The Family Hotel

Sited in a strikingly arid landscape, Tibooburra frequently registers the highest temperatures in New South Wales. Offering welcome relief for thirsty locals and travellers is The Family Hotel.

The Family Hotel
Briscoe Street, Tibooburra
New South Wales
(08) 8091 3314

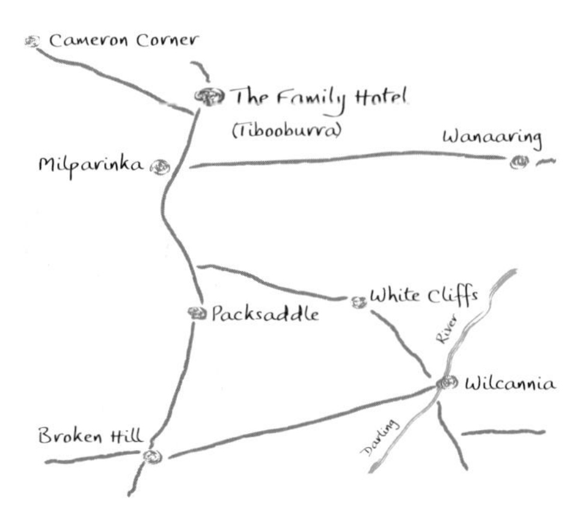

Built by Francis Bladen in 1883 of locally quarried sandstone, Tibooburra's Family Hotel is one of two pubs in this remote corner country town. The town's other hotel, The Tibooburra, is generally referred to as the 'Two Storey'.

The Family was once part of the web-like Cobb & Co network where passengers gained respite from the rough and tumble of stage coach travel, and horses were changed for the next leg of the journey. Even today the old horse stables are still located out the back of the pub.

Tibooburra was established at the height of the gold rush. First named 'The Granites' after the ancient granite tors which stand almost fortress-like surrounding the village, Tibooburra was originally part of the Albert Goldfields which was centred around Milparinka, about 40 kilometres to the south. Cattle King Sidney Kidman set up the first ration store on the new goldfield.

Fronting the town's main street with a shady verandah to sit and relax, the hotel is a substantial building, its massive sandstone block walls providing a feeling of permanence. Inside there are two bar rooms, along with a foyer with an open fire. There are a number of other rooms as well.

Adorning the walls of the pub are a collection of original murals painted by well-known artists Clifton Pugh, Russell Drysdale, Max Miller and Ric Amor. All were regular visitors to the corner country – as well as the hotel – being inspired by the region's rugged, desolate landscapes.

12-2 PM COUNTER
SOUP OF THE DAY 6.00
PASTA OF THE DAY
ROAST OF THE DAY
FISH IN BEER BATTER 16.00
FISHERMANS' BASKET 20.00
CHICKEN KIEV 18.50
SILVERSIDE & WHITE SAUCE N/A
SIDE DISH SALAD(SM)
VEGETABLES
EGGS
RUMP
PORK CHOPS
LAMB CHOPS
CHICKEN BREAST
*Served with Vegetables or Chips & Salad *
CHOICE OF SAUCES
MUSHROOM GRAVY
PEPPER DIANNE
2.00
HOME SWEET HOME
SES
HAROLD
AGFAIR 2006
Love the taste.
AUSTRALIA'S FAVOURITE PREMIUM LIGHT
LAGER

THE FAMILY HOTEL

Pugh's Pub

Clifton Pugh, who died in 1990, was one of Australia's best known painters, widely regarded for his expressionist landscapes and portraiture. He was a three-time winner of the Archibald Prize.

During the 1960s and 70s, Pugh, along with other popular artists of the day, spent considerable time at Tibooburra. Pugh also ran painting workshops around the town, using the desert vastness of the area as subjects. It has been said that Tibooburra – but probably more so The Family Hotel – was Pugh's second home!

Pugh owned the The Family Hotel for a period, although he was not the owner of the pub at the time the walls were used by the artists; it was run by Barney Davie, a mate of Pugh's. One story goes that Pugh was stranded at the pub during wet weather. He became bored after awhile and started doodling on the walls. This was in 1969. This no doubt set the scene with Pugh leaving a number of artworks, along with a bacchanalian mural on one of the walls. Pugh also painted a devil with a beard which bore a striking resemblance to his ex-wife's boyfriend. There are also two nude murals who were said to be the pub owner's daughters.

... some were painted in exchange for a few beers but when Pugh hit the big time, becoming rich and famous, he ended up buying the pub.

The Junction Hotel

A welcoming sight for almost 100 years, this charasmatic bush boozer has served beer to gold prospectors, graziers, drovers and throngs of travellers who have ventured out into the remote Gascoyne.

The Junction Hotel
Carnarvon Road, Gascoyne Junction
Western Australia
(08) 9943 0504

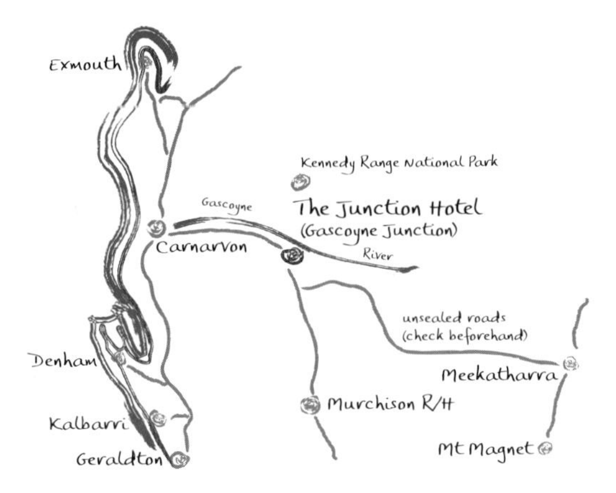

Originally licenced in 1911, The Junction Hotel was the second licenced hotel in the district, although there had been numerous sly grog shops operating around the district plying drink to the gold miners and drovers in the area.

Percy Ayliffe, who had previously been the proprietor of the Eurannie Wayside Inn near Mt Augustus, was the hotel's first licensee in the newly gazetted township of Killili, later renamed Gascoyne Junction in 1939.

In these early days as gold mining declined and droving increased, the sight of the hotel's white roof amongst the gum trees would have no doubt been a welcome sight to weary travellers, as at the time there was little at Killili other than the pub, Cox's store and the Roads Board Office.

Disposing of empty beer bottles was always a problem in remote towns, so one enterprising publican in the 1920s started stacking the bottles around the perimeter of the hotel to create a fence. This practice continued until the 1950s before the fence was demolished.

In 1955 the hotel became freehold when the owners of Jimba Jimba Station found it was becoming a burden to their pastoral interests. It was bought by John Carter, who subsequently went about demolishing the town's old police station, using the salvaged material to improve the hotel.

Located not far from the river, the hotel has been inundated by floods, but the enduring corrugated iron pub has continued to trade from the same location now for almost 100 years.

GU·72
33-095
C·10913
W.A. The Golden State
DN·8151
FARM
LUNCH/SNACK
Steak/Hamburger $11.50
With chips $15.00
Extra's egg/bacon $2.00
Bacon+egg sandwich $9.00
Basket Chips
Bucket Chips
Tea /Coffe
SWAN
SWAN

The Junction Hotel

MOTORS
ONLY

EMU
BITTER
The
Junction Hotel

The Logan Pub

This Victorian goldfields pub has become a bit of an institution. Standing on the edge of the famous 'Golden Triangle', it's been host to many a fortune seeker over the last century.

The Logan Pub
Wimmera Hwy, Logan
Victoria
(03) 5496 2220

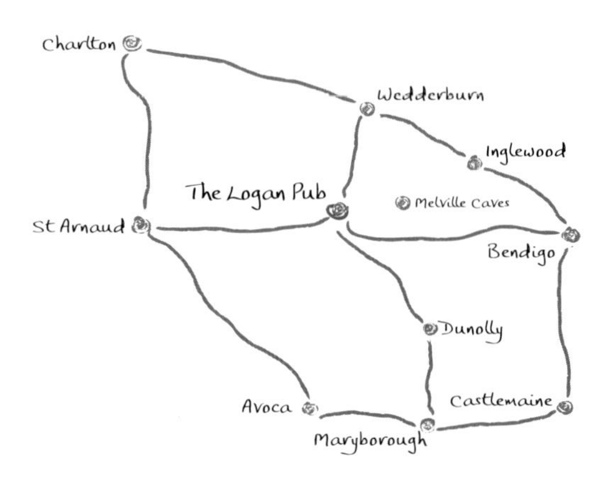

The tiny hamlet of Logan is located in Victoria's famous 'Golden Triangle'. Bordered by the towns of Wedderburn to the north, Dunolly to the south and Inglewood to the east, 'The Triangle' has contributed 90% of the world's largest gold nuggets. Welcome Stranger, the world's largest nugget, was found at Moliagul, near Dunolly, in 1869. Even today valuable nuggets are still being unearthed in the area, making it popular with prospectors.

With the discovery of gold came outlaws. Bushranger Francis McCallum, alias 'Captain Melville' was notorious for his highwayman feats in the area during 1851. Nearby Melville Caves is said to have been used as a hideout by the outlaw, however, he was a little early for a beer as the first pub at Logan wasn't built for another four years!

The weatherboard clad and corrugated iron roofed hotel is the third pub to be sited in Logan, although there has been a pub here since the mid 1850s when gold prospectors converged on the area. The hamlet's first pub was moved to a nearby sheep property and used as shearer's quarters after the grazier bought the pub – he was becoming tired of trying to get his inebriated shearers back to work. Subsequently, a second hotel was built on the site but burnt down. The third and current building was built in 1910.

Inside this friendly little hotel there is a small bar room off to one side while a larger room houses a pool table and a dining room. The walls of the front bar host a collection of odds and ends from axes to pen sketches.

WEEKLY
TIMES
For
Sale
VB
VICTORIA
BITTER

THE LOGAN PUB
THE PUB IN THE SCRUB
Bar & Meals
FUEL

COUGAR

COFFEY'S FIRST
SHOW WINNING AXE
Bairnsdale Show 2000
275mm STANDING BLOCK CHAMPIONSHIP
First

WEEKLY TIMES

The Pub in the Paddock

One of Tasmania's oldest country pubs, the St Columba Falls Hotel, is essentially a pub in the middle of a paddock. It was originally a guesthouse for visitors to the falls before becoming a hotel.

St Columba Falls Hotel
St Columba Falls Road
Pyengana, Tasmania
(03) 6373 6121

Tucked away in the tranquil Pyengana Valley is the charming St Columba Falls Hotel, otherwise known as The Pub in the Paddock. Apart from a delightful location – within close proximity to St Columba Falls – the hotel boasts a unique resident, Priscilla the beer-drinking pig. Boy, this swine really knows how to drink! She can knock back a stubbie in about four seconds. Even though it's only water with a little bit of added beer slops, it's still an impressive feat.

The heritage-listed pub dates back to the 1880s and some sections of the original structure remain. Built as a residence for the Terry family and their 12 children, the home first operated as a B&B for visitors to the falls before eventually becoming a hotel. It gained its licence in 1901.

The name 'Pub in the Paddock' is said to have originated from mail that was addressed to the hotel in the early days. Many of the senders either didn't know, or couldn't remember, the pub's official title so simply sent letters addressed to 'The Pub in the Paddock'. The name stuck.

The pub itself consists of a cosy timber-lined front bar with the obligatory open fireplace in one corner. This is a popular spot on those chilly Tassie nights. Out the back there is a large dining room – this time with a slow combustion heater – and off this there are a number of accommodation guestrooms. A small verandah is attached to the front of the original entrance way and a grassed area also has seating for those sunny afternoons.

PUB IN THE PADDOCK
(ST. COLUMBA FALLS HOTEL)

HOUSE POLICY
TIGER LILY

Tiger Tales

Pyengana is about 25 kilometres inland from the fishing and holiday town of St Helens. The valley's lush green pastures are home to dairy cattle. There's even a small cheese factory here.

But in 1995 it was a frenzied scene with reporters and journalists converging on the sleepy valley after word spread that a Tasmanian Tiger, believed to have been extinct since the 1930s, had been purportedly sighted by a forestry ranger in a remote area of the valley. There had been a number of sightings of the thylacine here, but this one, coming from a ranger, seemed kosher.

According to the book, *Carnivorous Nights*, the ranger told the *Sydney Morning Herald* newspaper 'What I viewed for two minutes was about half the size of a fully matured German shepherd dog, he had stripes over his body from about half way down, and his tail was curved like a kangaroo's. ... He sniffed the ground, lifted his head and ran into the bush. He was a scrappy color like a dingo – that horrible sandy color that looks like he needed a bath.'

The sighting was apparently made near the St Columba Falls. Was it a hoax? The book goes on to say that the publican of the day allegedly paid a part-time forestry ranger $500 to say that he had seen the tiger in order to drum up business for the pub, which it did!

In December 1998 a group reported seeing what looked like a 'tiger' on the road between Pyengana and Weldborough.

PRISCILLA.
PRINCESS OF THE PADDOCK
Hi!
GEEZ I'M DRY
I'D LUV A BEER.

FINE TIME!
MRS. MAC'S

Tilpa Hotel

This corrugated iron gem sits on the banks of the Darling River south of Bourke. Just oozing with character, this pub is hard to go past as you wind your way along the famous inland river.

Tilpa Hotel
Darling Street, Tilpa
New South Wales
(02) 6837 3928

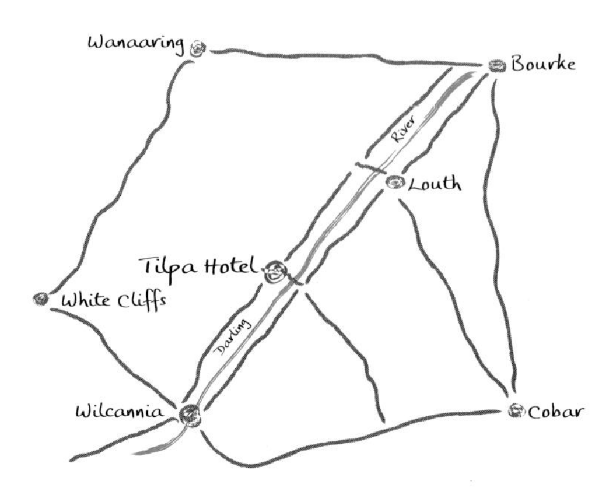

To many, the Tilpa Hotel is considered one of the last remaining true bush pubs. Established in 1894, the hotel grew from the river boat trade that once plied the Darling River. Pastoralism also added buoyancy to the local area, as it still does today. You'll more than likely be rubbing shoulders with cockies, shearers, rouseabouts and wool pressers in the pub's front bar.

Interestingly, the poet Harry 'Breaker' Morant once worked in the area, droving cattle and breaking horses before heading off to the Boer War and into the history books. His name is inscribed on the village's war memorial.

An observation from 1927 described the pub then as 'a wooden building with an iron roof consisting of a main portion containing a first class dining room, 2 parlours, 8 bedrooms and large wire gauze covered sleeping out space, also a detached building consisting of kitchen and second class dining room...'.

Today's Tilpa Hotel has changed little. This humble 100-odd year old attraction, made from corrugated iron and weatherboard with a concrete floor, is a great meeting place. Inside is a front bar and a dining room.

Local characters always have a few stories and tall tales from this part of the world. They may even let you in on the good fishing spots along the river, and if the monster heads of the Murray River Cod which adorn the pub's walls are anything to go by, the fishing here might be well worth a try!

No more violence
No more drink driving
PERMITTED BY LAW
IN THIS AREA
OF THE HOTEL
Keeping under 0.05
Enjoy a few...Not a few too many
Code of Practice
PUBLIC NOTICE
TILPA PUB
MY FAVORITE TIME
ORIGINAL SALTED
TOOHEYS NEW

STUBBIES
47.00

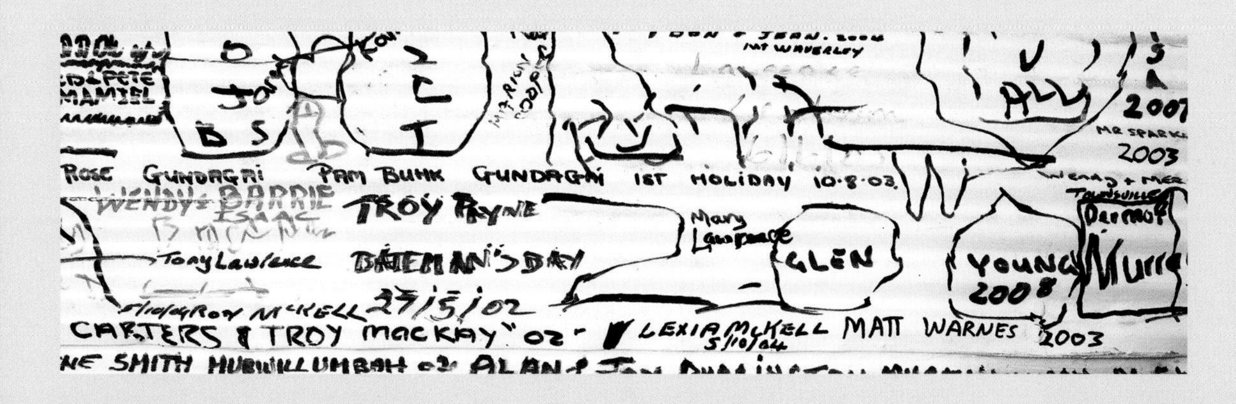

Walls of Graffitti

There aren't too many pubs where you can write your name on the wall with a permanent marker pen, but at the Tilpa Pub you can, and all for a good cause.

The corrugated iron walls inside the bar are covered with signatures, phrases, messages and poems. For a small fee, which is donated to The Royal Flying Doctor Service, visitors can pen their own poetry or prose, if they can find a space.

It's all good fun for a worthy cause.

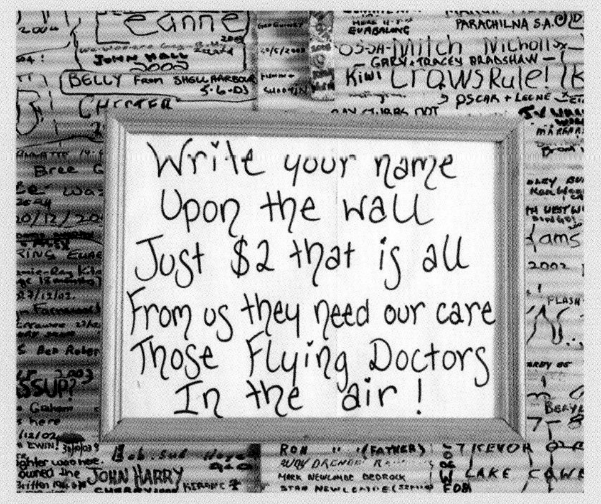

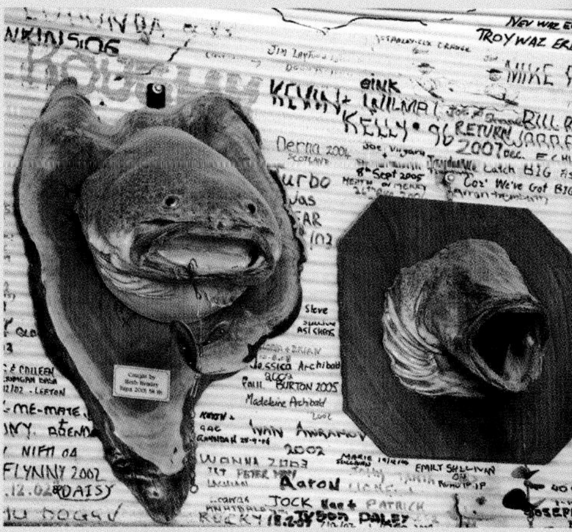

The Tilpa Pub is a much talked about destination for those travelling along the Darling River between Bourke and Wilcannia.

LP 9018
PROBATION
YUBA COUNTY CA
VICTORIA POLICE
N.S.W. POLICE
POLICE
VANCOUVER FIRE DEPT.
VANCOUVER FIRE 1886 DEPT.
WILLIAM CREEK HOTEL
Outback South Australia
FINE OLD TAWNY
HOUGHTON
JACOB'S CREEK
RIESLING
MAGNETS $ 5.00
TAWNY PORT BOTTLE $ 20.00
CUPS SMALL $ 5.00
FOR SALE
mentos
EVEREADY
SAVER 4 PACK
VALUE PACK 10
DURACELL
SMITHS
CRINKLE CUT
RYVITA

William Creek Hotel

Yaraka Hotel

William Creek Hotel

William Creek is one of the smallest towns in Australia and sits on the world's largest cattle station – the 24 000 square kilometre Anna Creek Station – which is almost half the size of Tasmania!

William Creek Hotel
Oodnadatta Track
William Creek
South Australia
(08) 8670 7880

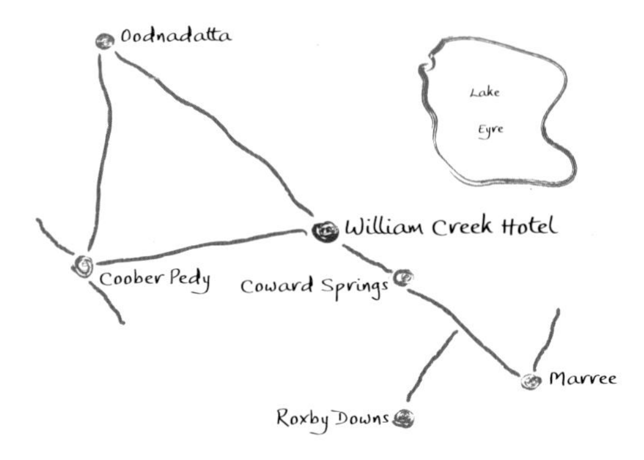

The hotel at William Creek is the only boozer on the Oodnadatta Track between Marree and Oodnadatta. Still largely in its original guise, the pub provides an insight into outback life and is filled, literally, to the rafters with unique mementos left over the years by tens of thousands of visitors. The rustic timber and corrugated iron building, dating from 1887, is like a visitors book. Over the years the walls have been covered with business cards, hand scrawled notes, bras, jocks and almost anything else which comes to hand.

William Creek was established along the Overland Telegraph Line and acted as a service point for both the line workers and camel strings operating along the route. When the railway reached here in 1885, it was seen as a vital watering and service point on the narrow-gauge line between Marree and Oodnadatta. The site had already been named in 1859 by explorer John McDouall Stuart after the second son of John Chambers, a pioneer pastoralist and a staunch supporter of Stuart's explorations.

The pub wasn't licenced as a hotel until 1935. Before this it was a boarding house, then became a store and, allegedly, an illegal wine bar.

The pub's painted corrugated iron walls reflect that unique character quintessential to bush pubs. With the closure of the hotel at Tarcoola, the William Creek Pub is the only corrugated iron hotel still trading in South Australia.

The pub's facade gives little indication of what awaits inside. Once through the enclosed screened

ALL MEALS INCLUDE
F.D.S.
DRAUGHT
WILLIAM CREEK HOTEL
OUTBACK SOUTH AUSTRALIA
mentos
KOSSECKI OFF ROAD
John Williamson

XXXX GOLD
AUSTRALIAN LAGER
WILLIAM CREEK HOTEL
XXXX GOLD
AUSTRALIAN LAGER
•ACCOMMODATION
•CAMPING GROUND
•DINING ROOM MEALS
•ICE COLD BEERS
•PETROL, DIESEL
•TYRE REPAIRS
XXXX GOLD
LAGER
GATEWAY TO SIMPSON DESERT & LAKE EYRE
Coopers
WILLIAM CREEK HOTEL
COLD COLD BEER
TYRES & REPAIRS
BBQ GAS, GROCERIES
BREAKFAST SERVED IN DINING ROOM!
NOW OPEN

WAROOKA MARINE & HARDWARE 88545007
AMPOL
RACING
Reeuwijk
holmatro
Chubb
JOHN LAWSON
POLICE
Nestlé
Peters
LIFE UP THE CREEK
Up this creek they love it
4WD
804

verandah, there's the front bar and dining room around the back, past the small pool room. The ornate – for a bush pub – front bar came from the Coward Springs Hotel, which was once situated further east down the track.

At the bar you're likely to meet locals from nearby cattle stations, fellow travellers exploring the Oodnadatta Track or heading to places further afield. There is also the constant flow of overseas tourists, many of them European backpackers who venture to this remote outpost to experience Australia's outback.

The Oodnadatta Track

The Oodnadatta Track passes through a mixture of plains and undulating countryside, running between Marree in the south and Marla on the Stuart Highway in the north. Largely following the route of the Old Ghan Railway, remnants and sidings of which feature prominently on the trip. Corrugations, potholes, loose stones, sand patches and lots of bulldust are constant companions, but in spite of this, it is generally passable to conventional vehicles. After rain, it is usually only suitable for four-wheel drives.

William Creek is located roughly one third the distance along the track from Marree.

The Old Ghan Railway Line was used for the last time in October 1980, but the William Creek Hotel is still serving travellers.

Yaraka Hotel

The focal point for the small outback Queensland community, the Yaraka Hotel would have been a rip roaring joint back in the town's heyday of the 1920s when the railway came to town.

Yaraka Hotel
Jarley Street, Yaraka
Queensland
(07) 4657 5526

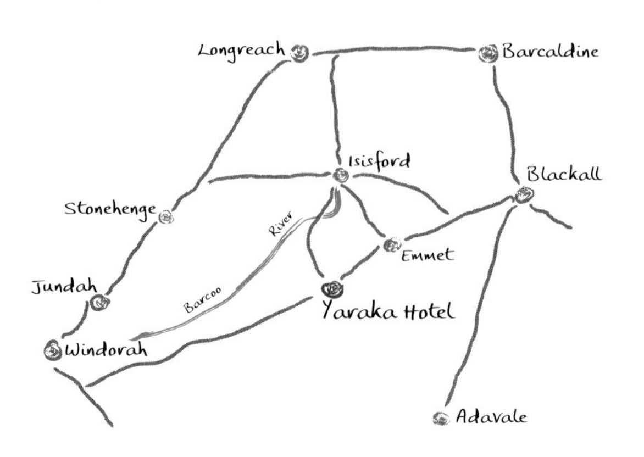

In 1910 work began on a 189 mile railway which would connect Blackall with Windorah, part of the Queensland Government's Great Western Railways Act. By 1917, after a number of delays, the line had reached Yaraka. It didn't go any further. Yaraka become 'the end of the line'.

At first Yaraka was a railway workers camp, but during the 1920s through to the 1930s it gained an air of permanency with stores, boarding houses, garage and in 1923, a police station. The first Yaraka Hotel was a flash affair, being a two storey building which was moved from Mt Morgan by train. It was located where the present day church stands and was destroyed by fire.

The single storey timber and iron building which acts as the pub today was first licenced to Mick Bauer sometime in the early 1930s. Over the ensuing years the pub changed hands a number of times until it ceased trading in 1987. It stayed closed until 1989 when it reopened and has continued to trade since.

The Yaraka Hotel is a good, honest, and above all, friendly outback watering hole. It's neat and tidy and not plastered with paraphernalia found in many outback pubs these days. Inside there is a long bar with a dining area located off to one side. Out through the back door is a beer garden with a separate accommodation block off this.

Today the railway line is quiet. The last train ran to Yaraka in 2007.

XXXX
LES THOMAS
LICENSEE
YARAKA HOTEL

XXXX
XXXX
SNACKS
Coca-Cola

Mount Up & Ride
BULLIEVE IT!
JUNDAH PUB
RAAF
A vaccinated horse is loved longer
RIGHT!
Cyclone
XXXX Our beer.
Crash in bed, instead.
BIRDSVILLE TRACK
XXXX
LIGHT BITTER
POWERS BITTER

XXXX

XXXX

XXXX
Our beer.
PUBLIC BAR

Index

ROYAL MAIL
HOTEL
LICENSEE: PETER YOUNG

YARAKA HOTEL
I SUPPORT MY LOCAL HOTEL
OUTBACK QUEENSLAND
PH (07) 4657 5526
TILPA HOTEL
UHF 35
TILPA, N.S.W.
PH: (02) 6837 3928
PYENGANA
TASMANIA
(03) 6373 6121
CREEK HOTEL
HOTEL
Bedourie
Channel Country
MIDDLETON HOTEL
Out Back Queenslan
THE Blue Heeler
HOTEL KYNUNA
HUNGERFOR
PHONE: (07) 4655 4093
ESTABLISHED IN 1859
Corner Hotel
Est. 1896
S.A. • N.S.W.
HISTORIC
NSW
OUTBACK AUSTRALIA
GLADSTONE HOTEL
WYANDRA
STH WEST QLD
PH (07) 4654 0273
HEBEL HOTEL
Cold Grog & Hot Pies
HEBEL QLD.
GRAND HOTEL
EST 1934
HERITAGE
HOTEL MUSEUM
Stan & Mary
PH: 08 8978 2489

AUSTRALIAN BUSH PUBS

Boiling Billy, a licensed imprint of
Woodslane Press Pty Ltd
Unit 7/5 Vuko Place
Warriewood NSW 2102 Australia
Tel: 02 9970 5111 Fax: 02 9970 5002
Email: info@woodslane.com.au
Web: www.woodslane.com.au

First published in hardcover by Woodslane Press in 2009
This paperback edition published by Woodslane Press in August 2010

Design Concept: Brent Occleshaw/Gooseboy Productions
Design & Layout: Craig Lewis/Boiling Billy Publications

Boiling Billy Publications
Locked Bag 1 Wyndham NSW 2550
Tel: 02 6494 2727
Email: info@boilingbilly.com.au
Web: www.boilingbilly.com.au

National Library of Australia Cataloguing-in-Publication entry

Author: Lewis, Craig (Craig William), 1966-
Title: Bush Pubs / Craig Lewis.
Edition: 1st ed.
ISBN: 9781921683329 (pbk.)
Subjects: Bars (Drinking establishments)--Australia.
Bars (Drinking establishments)--Australia--Pictorial works.
Hotels--Australia--Pictorial works.
Dewey Number: 725.720994

Printed and bound in China through Bookbuilders

All Boiling Billy and Woodslane Press titles are available for bulk and custom purposes. Volume copies of this and other titles are available at wholesale prices, and custom-jacketed and even mini-extracts are possible. Contact the Publishing Manager for further information, on